GCSE

Tracey Page
Alan Jones

Published in 2009 by:

Nelson Thornes Ltd
Delta Place
27 Bath Road
CHELTENHAM
GL53 7TH
United Kingdom

09 10 11 12 13 / 10 9 8 7 6 5 4 3 2

A catalogue record for this book is available from the British Library

ISBN 978 1 4085 0440 6

Cover photograph by Alamy/ Scott Hortop Travel
Illustrations by Andy Hammond
Page make-up by Hart McLeod

Printed in China by 1010 Printing International Ltd

Photo acknowledgements

Alamy: Paul Glendell / 6.4D; Stacey Richards / CO8; Stacey Richards / 8.1A; **Citizens
Advice Bureau**: 3.1A; **Community Legal Service**: 3.1B; **Corbis**: Miles / CO2; Pawel
Libera / 3.2C; Image Source / 4.3B; **Fotolia**: Sofia Papamitrou / CO7; Stephen Van
Horn / 8.2A; Diego Cervo / CO9; CO5; **Getty**: Tim Graham / CO4; **iStockphoto**: 1.1A;
CO3; CO6; 6.1A; 6.1C; 6.1D; 6.1E; 6.2A; 6.4B; 6.4C; 8.1B; **PA Photos**: PA Wire / 5.1A;
Photolibrary: Imagestate RF / CO1, 2.1A; **Rex**: 2.2B.

Contents

Nelson Thornes and AQA

Nelson Thornes has worked in partnership with AQA to make sure that this book offers you the best possible support for your GCSE course. All the content has been approved by the senior examining team at AQA, so you can be sure that it gives you just what you need when you are preparing for your exams.

◾ How to use this book

This book covers everything you need for your course.

Learning Objectives

At the beginning of each section or topic you'll find a list of Learning Objectives based on the requirements of the specification, so you can make sure you are covering everything you need to know for the exam.

| Objectives |
| Objectives |
| Objectives |
| Objectives |
| First objective. |
| Second objective. |

AQA Examiner's Tips

Don't forget to look at the AQA Examiner's Tips throughout the book to help you with your study and prepare for your exam.

AQA Examiner's tip

Don't forget to look at the AQA Examiner's Tips throughout the book to help you with your study and prepare for your exam.

AQA Examination-style Questions

These offer opportunities to practise doing questions in the style that you can expect in your exam so that you can be fully prepared on the day.

AQA examination questions are reproduced by permission of the Assessment and Qualifications Alliance.

Visit **www.nelsonthornes.com/aqagcse** for more information.

■ Why study Law?

According to the new AQA GCSE Law Specification, studying law gives students an understanding of the role of law in today's society. In addition, students acquire knowledge across a range of legal topics, and studying law helps to develop broader skills such as selection, analysis, critical thinking and decision making. Students will also develop an awareness of the rights and responsibilities of individuals.

If you have never studied law before, you are about to embark on an important journey. It is impossible to watch a news programme or read a newspaper and not be aware of how often the law has a part to play in all our lives. Whether it is buying something in a shop, being involved in a car accident, getting married, leaving a will or being prosecuted for a road traffic offence, the law will govern each and every aspect of these and many other situations.

■ What is this book about?

This book has been written specifically to cover the new AQA GCSE Law Specification. You will find, with its use of explanatory text, key cases, key word definitions, links to useful websites, test yourself questions and specimen examination material, that it will give you all the material you need to learn about the area of law involved and also how to turn that into examination success. You will also find a series of examiner's tips which will help improve your grade. The two authors are both experienced examiners and therefore are passing on good advice!

■ How you will be examined?

The Specification is examined in two written examinations. Candidates can enter one or both units in any examination series and question papers are designed to be accessible to candidates of all abilities.

Unit 1: The English Legal System consists of a written Paper lasting 1 hour 30 minutes. The paper carries 90 marks and is worth 50% of the total qualification. Candidates answer all the questions from Section A and one from a choice of two questions in Section B. Section A questions are generally short answer. Section B questions involve more detailed questions on a particular topic(s) based on stimulus material.

Unit 2: Law in Action consists of a second written Paper, also 1 hour 30 minutes, carrying 90 marks and worth 50% of the total qualification. Candidates answer two questions from a choice of four. The questions are problem based and cover the law of tort, crime, family, and rights and responsibilities.

■ Table of cases

Key cases and the pages upon which they appear are highlighted in blue.

■ Table of statutes

1 Introduction to law

In this chapter you will learn:

how to develop an outline understanding of the meaning of law and the necessity for a reliable system of law in a free society

how to develop an outline understanding of the legal differences between public law and private law

how to develop an understanding of the legal differences between civil and criminal law

how to develop an outline understanding of the court hierarchy including both first instance and major appeal courts.

■ Chapter contents

■ Definition of and need for law

There is no single correct definition of law, although most definitions will include similar elements. Put simply, law may be defined as: a set of compulsory rules about human behaviour, created and enforced by the **State**.

We need law to:

- provide minimum standards of acceptable behaviour
- provide a method of obtaining justice and resolving disputes
- promote order in society.

Key terms

State: defined territory covered by a system of government, e.g. the UK.

Source: where the law comes from/how it is made.

⊂⊃ links

See: Chapter 2 Criminal courts and processes; Chapter 3 Civil courts and processes; Chapter 5 Sources of English law; Chapter 6 The law of tort.

Starter activity

What makes laws different from your school/college rules? Discuss this with the person next to you and come up with a list of at least three ways in which they are different. Think in terms of the **source** of law; whom it applies to; what may happen if laws are broken.

1.1 Introduction to law

■ Classification of law

One way of classifying law is to divide laws into public or private law.

Public law

Public law means laws which affect the interactions between the State and its citizens. These laws may be about the way the government and laws are to be created (constitutional law); they may be about how government departments or public institutions are going to work in practice (administrative law); they may be rules about offences against the State (criminal law) or about human rights.

Private law

Private law is about how individuals interact with one another in specific situations, such as in business law, in family law and in civil wrongs such as negligence.

Another way of classifying law is as criminal or civil law.

Criminal law

Criminal law is made up of rules about offences which the State considers to be so important that they are said to be actions against the State as a whole; so the State (through institutions including the Police service; the Crown Prosecution Service and the Courts and Prison service) brings the person before a criminal court to answer the charge.

Civil law

Civil law is the same as private law as it is made up of rules about how individuals interact with one another in situations where an individual could bring a court case against them.

However, not all behaviour can be neatly classed as breaking either criminal or civil law. Some actions do both! For example, if you were chatting on a mobile phone while driving, and crashed into somebody, you would be breaking both criminal and civil law (negligence: see Topic 6.1).

A *Scales of justice*

AQA Examiner's tip

Practise using the correct terminology, based on whether you are discussing a civil wrong or a criminal offence. For example, don't confuse prosecuting with suing, or guilty with liable.

Did you know

Trespass is almost always a civil wrong, so signs that say 'Trespassers will be prosecuted' are incorrect – they should read 'Trespassers may be sued', although it doesn't have the same ring to it, does it?

B *Comparisons between criminal and civil law*

Comparisons	Criminal law	Civil law
Is about interactions between …	The State and its citizens	Individuals
The purpose is to …	Punish offenders	Put right wrongs against individuals
The names of the parties in a court case	**R** v defendant	**Claimant** v defendant
The process…	The State prosecutes	Claimant sues
Originally cases are heard in either…	The Magistrates' Court or the Crown Court	The County Court or High Court
The verdict in a trial is…	A person is found guilty or not guilty	A defendant is liable or not liable
The burden of proof is…	Beyond reasonable doubt (current test = if the jury is certain)	On the balance of probabilities
The outcome is…	A punishment if guilty	A remedy for the claimant
Examples are…	Murder and theft	**Tort** and family law

The UK courts

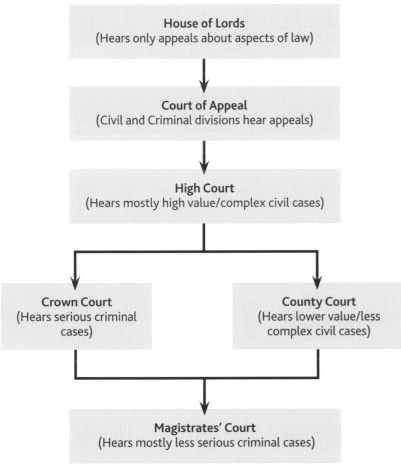

C *Hierarchy of UK courts*

You should now:

✔ know what law is and why we need it

✔ understand the differences between public and private law, and civil and criminal law

✔ know the names of the six UK courts in order of importance in the hierarchy

✔ know which of the courts are courts of first instance, and which are appeal courts.

Did you know ??????

The House of Lords is to be renamed the Supreme Court and will move to its own building on Parliament Square in October 2009.

∞ links

For further details about the Supreme Court, go to

www.justice.gov.uk/whatwedo/ supremecourt.htm

Revision questions

Close the textbook and see if you can remember the names and the order of the six main UK courts. Now see if you can work out from the diagram:

1 which court would hear a murder trial?

2 which court would hear a dispute about a faulty lawnmower?

3 which is the highest appeal court in the UK?

Have a look through your local newspaper and circle all the articles which are about law. See if you can identify whether they are civil law or criminal law by watching for key words.

What you should already know:

✓ criminal offences are actions said to be against the State (Chapter 1)

✓ the State brings the prosecution against the defendant (Chapter 1)

✓ the two main criminal courts are Magistrates' Courts and the Crown Court (Chapter 1)

✓ the outcome of a criminal trial is guilty or not guilty; if guilty a sentence is given (Chapter 1).

Chapter contents

Introduction to criminal law

In this chapter you will study how criminal cases are brought to court, and the legal processes before, during and after a criminal trial. You will also find out how criminal offences are classified in terms of seriousness.

If a person is suspected of having committed a crime, the police will investigate and charge the person with an appropriate offence. For minor offences the defendant will be sent a summons requiring them to attend the trial and for more serious offences police will arrest the defendant. The Crown Prosecution Service will decide if the charge is appropriate and also whether it is in the public interest to bring the case to trial. If so, they will prosecute minor crimes in the Magistrates' Court and more serious crimes in the Crown Court. This means that either a bench of magistrates (in a Magistrates' Court) or a jury (in the Crown Court) will decide the verdict. Magistrates also decide sentencing, but in the Crown Court the judge rather than the jury will decide sentencing.

Pre-trial issues 1

How criminal cases are brought to court

Criminal cases are brought to court in one of two ways, depending on the seriousness of the crime: by summons or arrest.

A summons is a document ordering the person to attend court, at a specified time, to answer a minor criminal charge.

Arrest (with or without a warrant) is for more serious offences. A warrant is a document, issued by magistrates, ordering the arrest of a named or described individual.

Powers of arrest without a warrant

These powers are outlined in the Police and Criminal Evidence Act 1984 (PACE), as amended by the Serious and Organised Crime Act 2005 (SOCPA).

By police

Police can arrest:

- anyone who is **about to** (or s/he has reasonable grounds for suspecting is about to) commit an offence
- anyone who is **in the act of** (or s/he has reasonable grounds for suspecting to be) committing an offence
- anyone who **has** (or whom s/he has reasonable grounds for suspecting has) committed an offence.

Provided s/he has reasonable grounds to believe that arrest is necessary, police can arrest:

- to gain correct name/address
- to prevent:
  - physical injury or damage to property
  - obstruction of the highway
  - public indecency
- to protect a vulnerable person
- to allow prompt investigation.

By private citizens

Other people may arrest:

- anyone who is **in the act of** (or whom s/he has reasonable grounds for suspecting to be) committing an indictable offence (including 'either-way' offences)
- where an indictable offence **has been** committed, anyone who is guilty of the offence or whom he has reasonable grounds for suspecting to be guilty of it, **provided** they believe it is not practical for a constable to make the arrest instead, and they have reasonable grounds for believing that it is necessary to prevent physical injury/ damage to property or to prevent them escaping before police can assume responsibility.

A *The Old Bailey*

If making a citizen's arrest, only reasonable force must be used in order to detain the person, and they must only be detained for the time it takes for a police officer to arrive, who must be called as soon as possible.

Role of Crown Prosecution Service

The CPS is the body responsible for:

- advising the police
- reviewing cases submitted by police
- determining charges (except minor cases)
- preparing and presenting cases in court.

Their decisions to prosecute are made based on:

1 whether there is sufficient evidence to provide a realistic prospect of conviction
2 whether it is in the public interest to do so.

Evaluation of CPS

- The CPS is **objective** in deciding if a case should be prosecuted, potentially saving time and money. The Police are likely to be more **subjective**, having been involved in the investigation.
- The CPS has been criticised for overspending on administration and for lacking independence, having to rely on police for information.

Classification of criminal offences

Criminal offences are classified according to seriousness, as either **summary**, **triable-either-way**, or **indictable**. The chart below outlines the key differences between them.

Key terms

Objective: seeing things from an independent or outside viewpoint.

Subjective: seeing things from an inside/personal viewpoint.

Summary: the least serious type of crime: see classification chart.

Triable-either-way: mid-range crimes: see classification chart.

Indictable: the most serious type of crime: see classification chart.

∞ links

For further information about the CPS see **www.cps.gov.uk**

B *Classification of criminal offences*

Classification	Seriousness	Court heard in	Decision-maker	Max. sentence	Example crimes
Summary	Least serious crimes	Magistrates hold summary trial	Magistrates/district judge determines both verdict and sentence	6 months imprisonment and/or £5,000 fine for single offence	Common assault; minor motoring offences
Triable-either-way offences	Mid-range seriousness	Either Magistrates' or Crown Court – magistrates and defendant decide which (see later)	As above if in Magistrates' Court or a jury in Crown Court	Up to max. for the crime in question (magistrates' powers limited to 6 months but may send to Crown Court for sentencing)	All forms of theft; ABH
Indictable	Most serious crimes	Sent to Crown Court by magistrates – for trial on indictment	Jury decides verdict and judge sentences if found guilty	As above	Murder; rape

Learning summary

You should now be able to:

know that crimes are classified as either summary, triable-either-way, or indictable offences

know who the CPS are and what their role is in the criminal justice system.

Pre-trial issues 2

Offences triable either way – deciding which court

The decision regarding the trial court for triable-either-way offences is initially made by magistrates, based on the likely sentence if the defendant were to be found guilty, as they can sentence only up to six months/£5,000 fine. However, even if they decide they are able to hear the trial, the defendant has the right to choose jury trial in the Crown Court instead.

Objectives

In this topic you will learn:

how to develop an outline understanding of how the decision is made regarding the trial court for triable-either-way offences

how to develop an outline understanding of the role of duty solicitors

how to develop an outline understanding of the granting of bail.

A Decision regarding trial court for either-way offences

(Flowchart content:)

Defendant pleads not guilty → Mode of trial hearing held in Magistrates' Court → Magistrates decide case *can* be heard there → Defendant can still choose Crown Court trial instead if they wish

Defendant pleads guilty → Trial heard in Magistrates' Court

Magistrates decide it *cannot* (based on likely sentence if found guilty) → Defendant has no choice – case will be sent to Crown Court

B Magistrates' Court

If magistrates find the defendant guilty of a triable-either-way offence and they consider that their sentencing powers are insufficient, they can send the defendant to Crown Court for sentencing.

The Duty Solicitor Scheme

At the police station, the scheme enables a person who has been arrested to receive free legal advice. This advice may be provided over the telephone if it is a minor offence.

At the Magistrates' Courts, a duty solicitor gives free legal advice on the defendant's first court appearance, after being charged with a criminal offence which carries a potential prison sentence.

Both schemes are funded by the Legal Services Commission.

Evaluation of duty solicitors

- Duty solicitors provide valuable *advice*, free of charge, but *representation* in court is not automatically free.

C A criminal behind bars

- In court, advice is not available for minor offences.
- At a police station, advice may be given by phone.
- Although criticised for giving an inferior service, duty solicitors must pass rigorous competence assessments to be accredited.

Bail

Police bail

Bail means the defendant is released until their trial. 'Street bail' may be given by police, to appear at a police station; or by a custody officer at the police station, following charge.

Court bail

Bail may also be granted by the Magistrates' Court. Under the Bail Act 1976, as amended by Criminal Justice Acts (CJA) 1988 and 2003, there is a **presumption that bail will be granted** unless there are good reasons to refuse it.

However, bail will be refused if there is a serious risk that:

- the defendant will fail to surrender
- they will commit further offences
- they will interfere with witnesses/obstruct justice

and the attaching of bail conditions would not avert this risk.

When deciding whether to grant bail, magistrates will consider:

- the nature and seriousness of the offence
- the likely sentence
- strength of evidence
- previous convictions/record
- community ties.

Conditions that may be attached to bail:

- a surety – a person responsible for ensuring you attend court and who may have to pay a specific sum if not
- reporting to a police station at specified intervals
- residence at a specific address
- curfew – may be enforced by electronic tagging
- restrictions – e.g. staying away from a specific person or place.

If a person fails to attend court (absconds) on the specified date they may be arrested.

D *On the run*

Did you know **??????**

The American meaning of bail is often confused with the UK meaning. In the UK bail is *not* the amount of money given to secure freedom until trial but is personal freedom until the trial.

Remember

If a person is accused of an offence which is classed as a triable-either-way offence, they have the right to choose trial by jury in the Crown Court if they plead not guilty. This applies even if the offence is a minor triable-either-way offence, e.g. theft of a box of cornflakes.

Remember

There is a presumption that bail *will* be granted, so it is up to the prosecution to show why it should not, rather than the other way around.

∞ links

See Work of Magistrates' Court and Crown Court later in this chapter.

See Topics 4.1 and 4.2 for details on juries and magistrates.

See Chapter 7 Criminal law for details of offences.

Learning summary

You should now be able to:

know how the decision is made regarding the trial court for triable-either-way offences

know the role of duty solicitors

know the factors and conditions surrounding the granting of bail.

2.3 Procedure in criminal trials

Criminal court trials

Magistrates' Court trial

Magistrates hear summary and either-way offences in summary trials. The vast majority of criminal trials (over 95%) are heard here, and most defendants plead guilty, meaning the magistrates will sentence them according to the circumstances of the crime. If a defendant pleads not guilty, the process is as follows:

- The prosecution representative (usually a solicitor, but may be a barrister) gives an opening speech and calls their witnesses and produces their evidence. Witnesses are examined, cross-examined, and re-examined if necessary.
- The defence representative repeats the above process of calling, examining and cross-examining witnesses.
- Some defendants represent themselves, especially if they are charged with a minor offence.
- Closing speeches by both representatives – summing up the key points of evidence.
- Magistrates retire to consider the verdict. Although all three magistrates will contribute to the discussion and the verdict, only the chairperson speaks in court to deliver the verdict.
- They will return a guilty verdict if they consider the case against the defendant is proved 'beyond reasonable doubt'.
- Sometimes a pre-sentence report by the Probation Service is required before sentencing.
- If found guilty, magistrates will sentence up to six months/£5,000 fine for a single offence or will send the defendant to the Crown Court if they consider their powers are insufficient.

Youth Courts

Youth Courts are held in the Magistrates' Court, for defendants aged 10–17 who have committed all but the most serious crimes, e.g. murder. There is no criminal responsibility for those below the age of 10. Youth Courts differ from adult courts in the following key ways:

1 There is a less formal procedure, with less formal language used in court so that the defendant can understand the proceedings and the legal professionals wear no formal clothing such as wigs or gowns, which may intimidate the defendant.

2 The bench comprises of specially trained magistrates, with at least one of each gender.

3 No press are permitted and names will normally not be published in order to protect the defendant's privacy and to prevent them from being known as a 'criminal', which may prevent them from reoffending.

4 The sentences available are tailor-made to the young offender, mainly in order to rehabilitate (prevent re-offending), rather than to punish.

Objectives

In this topic you will learn:

how to develop an understanding of the role of magistrates in summary trial and trial of either-way offences

how to develop an understanding of the roles of judge and jury in trying indictable offences, including offences triable either way

how to develop an outline understanding of sentencing and criminal appeals.

Remember

A person is innocent until proven guilty in UK courts – it is not for the defendant to prove his/her innocence, but for the prosecution to prove his/her guilt.

links

See Chapter 4 for information on the role of magistrates and jury, solicitors and barristers, judges.

Activity

Write a list of differences between trial in Magistrates' Courts and the Crown Court: remember to include differences in personnel, sentencing powers, representation by type of lawyer, types of offences heard.

5 A Youth offending team become involved when a young offender is charged with an offence and they provide a variety of perspectives as to the best way forward as they come from a variety of backgrounds.

Trial in the Crown Court

A jury in the Crown Court tries indictable offences and either-way offences sent by the Magistrates' Court. A judge will oversee the trial and determine sentencing if found guilty. The most famous Crown Court is The Old Bailey in London, where the most serious or high-profile cases are heard.

Only the most serious crimes are heard in the Crown Court and the process is as follows:

- jury is sworn-in
- prosecution opening speech and witnesses are examined; cross-examined and re-examined if necessary (by barristers or solicitor-advocates)
- defence repeats the above
- closing speeches
- jury retires to consider verdict
- guilty verdict if jury considers prosecution case proved 'beyond reasonable doubt'
- if guilty, judge passes sentence.

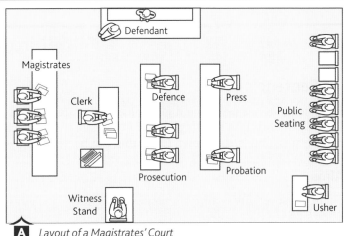

A   *Layout of a Magistrates' Court*

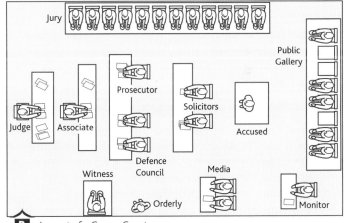

B   *Layout of a Crown Court*

C   *Evaluation of criminal court trials*

Magistrates' Court	Crown Court
Vast majority of criminal trials are heard here	Only the most serious cases are heard here and these can be complicated and/or traumatic
Find more people guilty than juries. However, most defendants actually plead guilty in magistrates' court	Juries acquit more defendants, possibly because they are less prosecution-minded than magistrates and more likely to be sympathetic
Cases are dealt with more quickly and cheaply	Trials take longer and are much more expensive
Procedures are much simpler and the sentences likely to be less severe. Sentences up to six months/£5,000 fine for a single offence	As procedures are more complicated, it is unusual for defendants to represent themselves and often both solicitor and barrister attend court and must both be paid

Learning summary

You should now be able to:

know the role of magistrates in summary trial and trial of either-way offences

know the roles of judge and jury in trying indictable offences, including offences triable either way.

AQA *Examiner's tip*

Study the court layout and personnel in each carefully so that you know who is likely to sit where.

Post-trial issues

Sentencing

If a defendant has been found guilty, by magistrates or by a jury, they will be sentenced. In the Magistrates' Court this will be decided by the magistrates, and in the Crown Court this will be decided by the judge.

Aims

There are several reasons for sentencing offenders, including:

1 retribution and denunciation – meaning punishment to fit the crime and showing society's disapproval
2 rehabilitation – meaning assisting in reform of the offender
3 reparation – to put right the wrong to society
4 deterrence – to deter others from committing the same crime
5 protection of society – to prevent society from being harmed.

Types of sentence

There are several options for sentencing offenders, including:

1 **Custody** – A prison sentence can be immediate or suspended. A suspended sentence will not have to be served unless further offences are committed within the given time period, and so acts as a deterrent. Custodial sentences are served in prison for those aged over 21, and in Young Offenders' Institutions for offenders aged 15 to 20 years old. Custodial sentences must be given only where the offence is so serious that this is the only justified sentence.

2 **Community orders** – These are sentences which will be served in the community. The orders are given to those aged over 16, where an offence is serious enough to justify it. Appropriate requirements will be attached to the order, the most common being: *unpaid work* of between 40 to 300 hours; *supervision* by the probation service; and a *programme* to address offending behaviour.

3 **Fines** – These are the most common sentence, given where the offence is not serious enough to merit a community penalty.

4 **Discharges** – *Absolute* discharges are given where no punishment is appropriate and *conditional* discharges are given where no punishment is given as long as specific conditions are met within a period of up to three years.

Magistrates' Association Guidelines on sentencing permit magistrates to make structured decisions, based on an entry point for the offence; maximum sentences and potential **aggravating** and **mitigating** factors (see next page). Their powers are to sentence up to six months' imprisonment and/or a £5,000 fine for a single offence. In the Crown Court, judges may sentence up to the maximum sentence for the crime, and in some cases there are **mandatory** sentences, e.g. life imprisonment for murder. Pre-sentence reports are generally obtained from the probation service before a decision is made.

Objectives

In this topic you will learn:

how to develop an outline understanding of the aims and factors in sentencing

how to develop an outline understanding of criminal appeals.

Activity

1 Go online to: www.cjsonline.gov.uk/offender/sentencing

Answer the following questions from the information on this site:

a Which body was created in 2004 to produce sentencing guidelines for criminal courts?

b Under what conditions can a judge depart from these guidelines?

c What is the sentence for:

  ■ a second serious sexual/violent offence

  ■ murder

  ■ third-time drug trafficking for class A drugs

  ■ third-time domestic burglary?

∞ links

For sentencing activities see: **www.magistrates-association.org.uk/about_magistrates/sentencing-examples.htm**, and for more on young offenders institutions see: **www.hmprisonservice.gov.uk/adviceandsupport/prison_life/youngoffenders**

Factors

Aggravating factors are those which make the offence and therefore the sentence, more severe. Examples include:

- seriousness of the crime
- racial motive – can add up to two years, depending on the crime
- antecedents – previous convictions/criminal record
- use of a weapon
- on bail when offence committed
- vulnerable victim.

Mitigating factors are those which make the offence and therefore the sentence, less severe. Examples include:

- first offence
- age of offender – either young or elderly
- offender shows remorse
- early guilty plea – can take up to one-third off sentence if made at earliest opportunity
- background, or other mitigating circumstances surrounding the offence.

Routes of criminal appeals

There are two **courts of first instance** in the criminal justice system: Magistrates' Courts and the Crown Court. There are four **appellate courts**, depending on the grounds for the appeal and where the original trial was heard: the Crown Court; the High Court; the Court of Appeal; and the House of Lords.

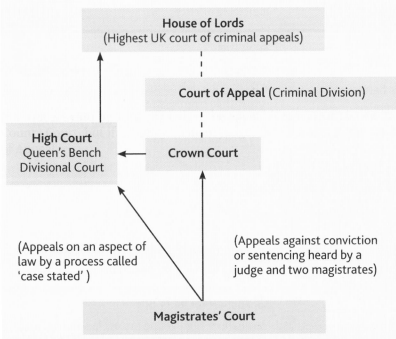

A *Hierarchy of criminal appeals*

Chapter summary

2

You should now be able to:

✔ explain the pre-trial processes and people in the criminal justice system

✔ explain the classification of criminal offences

✔ explain the key processes and people in criminal trials

✔ explain the post-trial issues of sentencing and appeals.

Revision questions

1. What is a summary offence, and where would it be tried?

2. What is an either-way offence, and where might it be tried?

3. What is the name of the process to determine where an either-way offence will be tried?

4. Who decides where an either-way offence is tried?

5. Who decides the verdict in trials for indictable offences?

6. What is a summons?

7. What are the differences between conditions under which a police officer can arrest and those where other citizens can?

8. In which court does a jury sit?

9. What types of crime would a jury hear?

10. Which body is responsible for prosecuting crimes?

11. What is a duty solicitor and where might you find one?

12. What are the *procedural* differences between cases of minor theft and minor motoring offences?

13. What does rehabilitation mean?

14. What is a Youth Court and what types of cases does it hear?

15. What maximum reduction in sentence can be given for an early guilty plea?

16. What does bail mean and who can grant it?

17. What conditions may be placed on bail?

18. What is a duty solicitor and where might you find one?

19. An appeal from the Magistrates' Court on a point of law will be heard in which court?

20. An appeal from the Crown Court against conviction will be heard in which court?

21. What does CPS stand for?

22. What is the maximum sentence available in a Magistrates' Court trial?

23. If the magistrates decide their sentencing powers are insufficient, what can they do about it?

24. What does mandatory mean, and what is the opposite of a mandatory sentence?

25. Where would a 16-year-old serve a custodial sentence?

26. What is the highest UK appeal court and what are the names of the judges who sit there?

27. What is the name of the Act of Parliament that governs powers of arrest?

28. Name a summary, a triable-either-way, and an indictable offence.

29. How does trial in a Youth Court differ from an adult trial?

30. What is the role of a judge in the Crown Court?

31. Why might a defendant choose trial by jury rather than by magistrates?

32. Why might trial by magistrates be chosen over a jury trial for either-way offences?

33. Where does the defendant sit, in the Magistrates' Court?

34. What are the five aims of sentencing?

35. What are the four main types of sentence?

36. What is a court of first instance?

37. Is a Magistrates' Court a court of first instance, or an appellate court, or both?

38. Is the Crown Court a court of first instance, or an appellate court, or both?

39. Name three aggravating factors in sentencing.

40. Name three mitigating factors in sentencing.

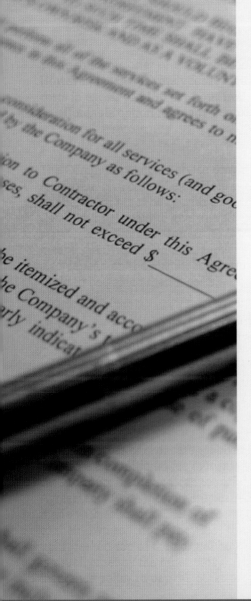

3 Civil courts and processes

■ What you should already know:

✔ civil cases are between individuals/companies (Chapter 1)

✔ the claimant sues a defendant to obtain a remedy (Chapter 1)

✔ the two main civil courts are the County Court and the High Court (Chapter 1)

✔ the outcome of a civil trial is that a defendant is liable or not liable (Chapter 1)

✔ examples of civil cases include: contract; tort; and family law (Chapter 1).

■ Chapter contents

■ Introduction to civil law

Many civil disputes can be resolved through the legal process including: torts such as negligence, nuisance and trespass (Chapter 6), family law and laws of succession (Chapter 8), contract and employment law (Chapter 9).

Before a civil dispute goes to court, there are several pre-trial issues to consider. First, it is wise to gain legal advice. If it is necessary to pay for legal advice and representation in court, there are several financing options available. Many civil claims can be resolved through negotiation between the parties, without the need for the case to go to court.

If the case does go to court, then a judge will decide the outcome and, if the verdict is in the claimant's favour, will award a remedy.

If either party is unsatisfied with the outcome of the trial, there is a civil appeals system.

Seeking legal advice

It is wise to seek legal advice for a civil dispute, if it cannot be resolved between the parties themselves. The following table outlines and evaluates the key sources of legal advice.

A *Citizens Advice Bureau*

B *Community Legal Service*

C *Sources of legal advice*

Source of advice	Features	Advantages	Disadvantages
Solicitors	Legal professionals Available throughout the UK Many offer low-cost initial interviews to advise on strength of case	Best known source of advice Legally qualified Will negotiate on client's behalf and send appropriate letters Can represent client in court if necessary	Probably the most expensive form of legal advice If relying on public funding (legal aid) then must find a solicitor with a contract for this type of work
Citizens Advice Bureau (CAB)	3,300 bureaux in UK Staffed mainly by volunteers Charitable organisations May have a qualified solicitor for certain issues	Advice is likely to be free Specialists in social/welfare problems, e.g. housing; employment; welfare benefits	Do not specialise in all aspects of law Appointment times may be delayed if high demand Unable to negotiate or represent clients in court
Law Centres	Available in larger towns and cities Staffed by salaried professionals Funded by government and charitable donations, e.g. from the Lottery	Specialists in social/welfare law issues Free advice to those on low income	Not available in smaller towns and villages – half are in London Demand for their services means there is a huge volume of work Rely on having sufficient resources
Websites	Websites exist for the purpose of giving general legal advice An example is the government-funded CLS website	Easily accessible advice Advice is accessed anonymously Free advice on general issues Often refer specific enquiries to another source	Not always a reliable source of information as websites change or are removed and anybody can set up a website offering inaccurate legal advice The advice given will be general and not relate to a specific person so further advice is likely to be required
Specialist bodies	Professional bodies often give legal advice for issues relating to their expertise, e.g. trade unions; insurance companies; motoring organisations	Specialist advice in their own area of expertise	Advice is limited to specific areas Quality of advice may vary

■ Negotiation

The vast majority of civil disputes are not settled through **litigation**, but through other methods of dispute resolution, particularly negotiation. Negotiation means that both parties or their representatives discuss the problem and seek to reach a mutually acceptable compromise solution.

Advantages over litigation include the fact that there is less bad feeling, as the solution is agreed by both parties, so there is no winner and loser. Costs are also kept to a minimum, as no court or representation costs are involved. It is also flexible, since any type of agreement can be made, not just the remedies granted by the courts.

Disadvantages include the fact that one party may be in a vulnerable position and may settle for a solution which is less beneficial than they would have received in court. Also, it is not guaranteed that a decision *will* be reached.

■ Financing advice and representation in civil cases

1 Private funding

Some solicitors offer *pro bono* services under certain circumstances. However, paying privately for legal advice and representation often costs in excess of £150 per hour from a solicitor. This is therefore not an affordable option for many people.

2 Public funding – legal help

The Community Legal Service provides public funding (legal aid) for certain civil cases. **Legal Help** is a type of assistance whereby a solicitor, or other body with a contract with the Legal Services Commission, is paid to give initial legal advice and assistance, and may write preliminary letters. This free funding is **means tested**, meaning only those on a very low income will qualify. Qualifying will also depend on the likelihood of winning the case and whether more is likely to be gained than it costs.

Excluded areas

Not all civil disputes will be publicly funded. Many key areas are excluded from this scheme and must be paid for either privately or through Conditional Fee Agreements (as described later). Such areas include small claims (those where under £5,000 is claimed) and personal injury cases (in negligence).

3 Conditional fee agreements

For many types of civil case, public funding is unavailable and therefore a conditional fee agreement may provide a way of bringing a case to court if a person cannot afford private funding. Conditional Fee Agreements (CFAs), commonly called 'no win, no fee' agreements, are made with solicitors. These agreements mean a claimant pays nothing to their own solicitor if they lose the case but has to pay a 'success/uplift fee' on top of the normal hourly rate if they win (although this is usually met by the other party). They must usually take out an insurance policy to pay the other party's costs, in case they lose.

Track allocation

Under the Civil Procedure Act 1997, cases are allocated to one of three tracks, depending on complexity and value.

1 Small claims track

- Claims are allocated to the small claims track if they are below £5,000 (or £1,000 for personal injury cases).

- These will be heard by the district judge of the County Court, usually in **chambers**. The procedure is informal, as the judge can adopt any method of dealing with the hearing that they consider to be fair, and they may ask questions of the witnesses before allowing anyone else to do so. The judge may limit the time that parties or witnesses have to give evidence.

- Costs are kept to a minimum and parties are encouraged to represent themselves, as legal costs will not be awarded to the **claimant** even if s/he wins. This does put some claimants at a disadvantage if the other party is a large company that is willing to meet its own representative's costs.

- There are limited appeals from small claims cases, mainly where the judge misapplied the law.

2 Fast track

- Claims between £5,000 and 15,000 will normally be allocated to the fast track within the county court.

- Parties are usually legally represented (by solicitors).

- Trials are held within six months of the claim form issue, and are limited to one-day hearings, so costs are kept as low as possible.

- Cases are managed by judges (usually circuit judges), who determine timetables and determine issues such as which witnesses will be called and control costs.

3 Multi-track

- Claims over £15,000 will be allocated to the multi-track, which is heard in either the County Court or the High Court, depending on complexity and value.

Trial in County Court

The County Court deals with small claims; fast track and multi-track claims in contract and tort cases; undefended divorce cases; bankruptcy cases; family law cases; probate (wills). The trial process is as follows:

- claimant representative's opening speech: claimant's witnesses are examined, cross-examined and re-examined (usually by solicitors)

⊖⊖ links

For more detail on description of district and circuit judges, see Chapter 4.

For more detail on civil remedies in tort, see Chapter 6.

For an interactive guide to civil appeals, see:
www.hmcourts-service.gov.uk/infoabout/appeals/index.htm

A *A County Court (This photograph has been posed by models. It is not of actual people, or meant to be representative of actual people who have been involed in court business or court cases.)*

- this process is repeated by the defendant's representative and witnesses
- defendant's and claimant's representatives' closing speeches
- the judge gives judgment – whether the defendant is liable or not
- if liable, a remedy will be granted to the claimant.

Remedies

Damages is the correct term for money compensation. A claimant has the right to be awarded damages if a civil wrong has been committed. Damages are awarded for losses incurred because of the wrong.

Injunctions are granted at the discretion of the court. They are court orders, preventing a person from, or compelling a person to, carry out a specific activity, e.g. to stay away from a specified place or person.

Civil appeals

The routes of appeal depend upon the court in which the case was originally heard, and also the level of judge who heard it:

> **Remember**
>
> Magistrates' Courts also have limited civil jurisdiction, e.g. in their Family Proceedings Courts, dealing with issues such as adoption and responsibility for children.

> AQA **Examiner's tip**
>
> Remember the key differences between small claims cases and fast track cases in the County Court.

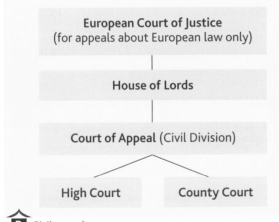

B *Civil appeals*

C *Royal Courts of Justice*

If a trial is heard by a district judge, the appeal is to a circuit judge in County Court, but if heard by a circuit judge, the appeal is to the Court of Appeal.

Learning summary

You should now be able to:

know the places where a person can find legal advice

understand about negotiating settlements

know the three ways of financing civil cases

know the three-track allocation system for civil cases

know the procedure in small claims and fast track cases in county court

understand the remedies of damages and injunctions

understand the civil appeals system.

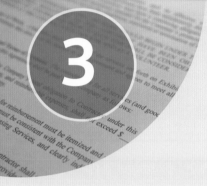

Chapter summary

3

You should now:

✔ know the places to find legal advice

✔ understand negotiation in civil cases

✔ know the ways a civil case can be financed

✔ understand track allocation in civil cases

✔ know the procedure in small claims and fast track cases

✔ understand the remedies available in civil cases

✔ understand the civil appeals system.

Revision questions

1 What are the main advantages of getting legal advice from a solicitor?

2 Why might advice from a solicitor not be an option for some people?

3 Describe two different ways of paying for legal advice in a negligence case.

4 What are the problems you may come across if you rely on websites for legal advice?

5 Why are most civil disputes settled through negotiation?

6 What is the main advantage of conditional fee agreements?

7 Other than personal injury, what is another type of case that will not receive public funding?

8 What are the differences in procedure between small claims and fast track cases?

9 How does the small claims procedure encourage claimants not to have solicitors to represent them?

10 Which track would a claim concerning a faulty toaster be allocated to and why?

11 Name the two types of judge who may hear County Court trials.

12 In what type of situation might a claimant want an injunction rather than damages as a remedy?

13 Who would hear a civil appeal from the decision of a district judge in the County Court?

14 Name the Act of Parliament which created the three-track system.

15 What is meant by Legal Help?

16 What are the major areas of work undertaken by the County Court?

17 What does the term 'means tested' mean?

18 What is the correct name for the process of bringing a case through the courts?

19 What are conditional fee agreements commonly known as?

20 When a solicitor's initial advice is publicly funded, what is the name for this type of assistance?

4 · People in the law

What you should already know:

✔ solicitors are providers of legal advice to the public (Chapter 3)

✔ magistrates work in the Magistrates' Court, hearing predominantly minor criminal trials (Chapter 2)

✔ juries operate in the Crown Court, hearing serious criminal trials (Chapter 2)

✔ district judges are found in Magistrates' Courts and County Courts (Chapters 2 and 3).

Chapter contents

Introduction to people in the law

In this chapter you will learn about the key professionals and lay people who perform roles within the justice system.

The key people who work in the civil and criminal justice systems may be classed as either lay people or legal professionals. Lay people are those who are not legally qualified and are not paid, other than expenses. These are magistrates and juries. Legal professionals are legally qualified and are paid. These are solicitors and barristers (the legal profession) and judges.

Virtually all criminal trials are decided by **lay people**: either juries or magistrates.

■ Juries

Juries are ordinary members of the public who are summoned to jury service (usually in the Crown Court) and must attend unless they have been officially disqualified or have been granted a deferral or excusal. Jurors are unpaid but can claim loss of income up to a designated maximum, reasonable travel costs and meal expenses. However, not everyone qualifies to be on a jury.

Qualification/disqualification

There are three qualifications for jurors, outlined in the Juries Act 1974 (amended by the Criminal Justice Act 2003):

1 Jurors must be aged between 18 and 70.
2 They must have been resident in the UK for a minimum of five years since the age of 13.
3 They must be entered on the **electoral register**.

Even if a person meets these three qualifications, they may actually be disqualified from serving on a jury.

This happens if they:

1 are currently on bail pending a criminal trial
2 have ever been given a custodial sentence of over five years
3 have been sentenced to custody or a community penalty within the last ten years
4 are mentally ill.

Selection

Jurors are selected at random from the electoral register, by computer at the Central Summoning Bureau. If summoned, jury service is a legal obligation. Twelve names will be selected by ballot in court. A juror may be challenged if they are known to anyone in the court or there is other cause, e.g. bias. Jurors are sworn in, taking an oath to give a true verdict.

Deferral/discharge

Any person can ask to have jury service **deferred**, or to be discharged from jury service. A discharge will not be granted if service can be deferred (put off to a later time). Deferral, for up to six months, will usually be allowed by the judge for a good reason, e.g. an exam or pre-booked holiday.

A potential juror can be discharged if, for example:

- they are not physically capable of sitting in court
- their command of English is not sufficient for court proceedings
- they have a long-term disability, such as blindness.

Objectives

In this topic you will learn:

how to describe and evaluate the qualification, selection and role of juries in the English legal system.

Key terms

Lay person: not legally qualified or paid.

Electoral register: electronic list of people registered to vote.

Deferred: put off to a later time.

Unanimous: all agree with the decision.

AQA *Examiner's tip*

Quoting appropriate Acts of Parliament and cases to illustrate your answers will increase your marks.

Members of the armed forces will be discharged if their absence from duty would prejudice the service.

The jury's role in criminal and civil trials

A *The role of the jury*

Role in criminal trials	Role in civil trials
A jury of 12 will decide the verdict in serious criminal cases (triable-either-way or indictable offences) in the Crown Court	Juries don't routinely hear civil cases but may be called on to decide cases of false imprisonment, malicious prosecution or defamation. They may also have to decide the cause of death at a Coroner's Court
Listen to the evidence and decide the facts	Listen to the evidence and decide the facts
Ask the judge to explain things, by sending a note through the court clerk	Ask the judge to explain things, by sending a note through the court clerk
Discuss the evidence and the verdict with the other jury members Jury deliberations are secret, so they cannot talk about the case to anyone outside of the jury room, where all jury members must be present. Only the 12 jurors are allowed in the jury room under the Contempt of Court Act 1981. This prevents a deaf person from sitting on a jury as they would not be permitted to take an interpreter into the jury room	Discuss the evidence and the outcome with the other jury members
Apply the law, as explained by the judge, to the facts, to reach a verdict of guilty or not guilty	Apply the law, as explained by the judge, to the facts, to reach a verdict of liable or not liable and, if required, decide on the amount of damages payable if liability is established
Juries must try to be **unanimous** in their verdict. However, after just over two hours, the judge is permitted to accept a majority verdict of a minimum of 10:2	
Deliver the verdict. The foreman (spokesperson elected by jury) delivers the verdict and the jury is discharged	Deliver the verdict. The foreman (spokesperson elected by jury) delivers the verdict and the decision regarding the amount of damages (compensation) to be awarded This is a notoriously difficult decision for them and they may award large sums of money which are out of proportion to the wrong committed, resulting in an appeal

∞ **links**

See Chapter 3 for a reminder of how the trial proceeds.

∞ **links**

Launch the interactive guide to jury service for further information on selection and role of juries:
www.juror.cjsonline.gov.uk/

Compare the role of a judge and jury in the Crown Court

A judge's role is to:

- keep order in the court
- make rulings concerning the law and the admissibility of evidence
- sum up the main facts of the trial and the legal arguments
- give an appropriate sentence if the jury finds the defendant guilty.

Evaluation of juries

There are advantages and disadvantages to juries.

B *Evaluation of juries*

Advantages of juries	Disadvantages/criticism of juries
Public confidence – many polls indicate that the public are confident that juries will reach the correct decision	It is difficult to evaluate whether juries reach the right decisions, using the right processes, due to the secrecy of the jury room and the fact that they are not required to give reasons for their verdicts
Having a jury keeps proceedings clear to the ordinary person and avoids the danger that the language used in court will become unintelligible to ordinary people, as everything must be explained in terms the jury (and therefore the defendant and everyone else) will be able to understand	They may reach their decisions by unauthorised methods and nobody would know if it were not made known to the court at the time. For example see the case of R v Young in 'Key cases'
Having twelve different viewpoints/strengths helps in making unbiased decisions. It is unlikely that ten out of the twelve would be biased or that they would all vote a certain way purely because of threats or expectations on them	Jurors may be influenced by media in a high-profile case and may have already decided their opinion as to innocence or guilt when hearing about the alleged crime. They may also be influenced in the jury room by a forceful spokesperson or in the court by an eloquent lawyer, rather than purely by the evidence
Juries represent the defendant's 'peers', meaning ordinary people, like them. They will come from a variety of backgrounds and experiences and skills, as they have been randomly selected. Judges do not generally represent the public in the same way, with most coming from a narrow, often privileged section of society	Jurors may not fully understand legal or technical points made during the trial. There is no test of basic understanding of verbal or written communication
Juries are able to make decisions based on their conscience and are more likely to vote according to common sense or a sense of justice than a legal professional would, who may stick exactly to the wording of the law even if it means an unjust result (see Bushell's case in 'Key cases' opposite)	**Perverse verdicts** are based on **subjective** opinion regarding justice and may lead to an outcome which our law-makers did not intend. It makes the outcome at the whim of that individual jury and may mean that there is a different verdict in a similar case, with a different jury. See R v Blythe in 'Key cases'
	Jury service is inconvenient for many jurors and much of their time is spent waiting around for a suitable trial. Because of this, some may rush through their decision to bring the trial to an end more quickly
	Jurors may be 'nobbled' or threatened to make sure they vote a certain way. They may also be traumatised by the evidence they are required to see and hear

Bushell's case (1670)

The case confirms that juries have the right to decide verdicts according to their own conscience.

R v Young (1995)

Jurors reached the verdict by communicating through a ouija board with the murder victim, resulting in a re-trial!

R v Blythe (1998)

Example of a 'perverse' jury verdict – a man was acquitted of cultivating cannabis to ease the suffering of his wife who had multiple sclerosis, despite clear evidence the offence had been committed.

Activities

1 Could the following sit on a jury:

a the mother of a young baby

b a deaf person

c a person who went to prison for six months, ten years ago

d a homeless person?

2 **Evaluation of juries**

Discuss the jury system with somebody near to you. Can you think of any reasons why the jury system is a good way of deciding serious criminal cases? Can you think of any reasons why it might be easier to have a judge to make these decisions? Compare your answers to the advantages and disadvantages mentioned here and try to think of some which are *not* mentioned.

AQA Examiner's tip

There is no set list of 'right' answers to *any* evaluation question. The examiner will accept any valid point that you can argue well. Make sure that when you name an advantage or disadvantage, however, that you also explain *why* this is an advantage or disadvantage of the system.

Learning summary

You should now be able to:

know that jurors are randomly selected from the electoral register and not everyone qualifies to be a juror

know that a jury's main role is to decide the verdict in Crown Court trials

know that juries may be called to sit on civil trials in limited circumstances.

■ Magistrates (also called Justices of the Peace/JPs)

There are over 30,000 magistrates throughout the UK, hearing over 95% of all criminal trials.

Selection and appointment

A potential magistrate applies to the Magistrates' Court. Applications are sifted by a Local Advisory Committee, which invites applicants for interview based on the criteria in the Justice of the Peace Act 1997:

- Applicants must be aged between 18 and 70 (although over 65s are unlikely to be appointed).
- The need must be taken into account for a balanced bench to represent the local community.
- Certain professionals are ineligible, including members of the police service.
- Applicants with criminal convictions or bankrupts may be disqualified.

There are six qualities sought in potential magistrates:

1 good character
2 understanding and communication
3 social awareness
4 maturity and sound temperament
5 sound judgement
6 commitment and reliability.

The second interview consists of practical decision-making activities and successful candidates will be passed to the Lord Chief Justice who will recommend them for appointment by the Lord Chancellor.

Role of magistrates

Magistrates must commit to sitting for a minimum of 26 half-days per year, although most exceed this. Employers are legally obliged to release them for a reasonable time to perform their duties.

They usually sit as a bench of three, with a chairperson and two 'wingers'. The chairperson is the only one who will speak in court. The bench will retire to discuss the verdict in a similar way to juries and the chairperson will deliver that verdict in court.

- Magistrates hold summary trials for summary and either-way offences. They listen to the evidence and decide a verdict. However, unlike a jury, their role also includes sentencing those found guilty.
- Their sentencing powers are up to 6 months custody and/or £5,000 fine for a single offence.
- They are advised on the law by a Legal Adviser/Court Clerk, who is also responsible for training, court administration and paperwork.
- They carry out many administrative tasks, e.g. bail hearings (see Chapter 2); granting arrest and search warrants (often from home);

A   A bench of magistrates

∞ links

See Chapter 1 classification of offences, and Chapter 2 for classification of crimes and role of Magistrates' Court, and District judges later in this chapter.

For further information about the selection and role of magistrates, go to: **www.magistrates-association. org.uk**

Click on the Youth site for an interactive guide, the layout of courts, and fun things to do, e.g. word searches.

transferring indictable offences to Crown Court; committals for sentence to the Crown Court, if they find a defendant guilty but their sentencing powers are insufficient.

- A trained panel of JPs may sit in the Youth Court to hear all crimes by young offenders between 10 and 17 except the most serious, e.g. murder which are held in the Crown Court. The Youth Court proceedings are less formal; with no press permitted and sentences are based primarily on rehabilitation (see Chapter 2).

- Specially trained JPs sit in civil proceedings in the Family Proceedings Court for matters such as judicial separation, adoption and maintenance.

- Two JPs sit with a judge to hear appeals from the Magistrates' Court, in the Crown Court.

Evaluation of magistrates

Magistrates are sometimes called the 'backbone' or the 'workhorse' of the criminal justice system because they hear the vast majority of all criminal cases.

AQA *Examiner's tip*

Remember that magistrates have a role to play in *all* criminal cases: trying summary offences; determining mode of trial/trying either-way offences; deciding on bail/remand; and transferring indictable offences to Crown Court. Make sure you also know their role in civil proceedings.

Key terms

Case-hardened: magistrates may see the same types of case on a regular basis and may hear the same kinds of defences or excuses.

B *Evaluation of magistrates*

Advantages	Disadvantages/criticisms
There are thousands of committed volunteers who willingly give up their time to serve the community	Some benches have been criticised as being unrepresentative of the community, with too many middle-aged and middle-class people appointed. (Although it could be counter-argued that they can only appoint from those who apply and meet the criteria and many either do not know they could apply or their work does not permit them to)
Magistrates are more representative of, and have more knowledge of, local communities than judges	Magistrates may become **'case-hardened'** as they see cases on a regular basis whereas a jury will hear only one case and judge it purely on its own merits
A bench of three allows for a balanced view	Magistrates have been criticised for believing the police version of events too readily
The fact that there are few successful appeals indicates they reach correct decisions most of the time	Magistrates are slower at decision-making than a district judge as they have to discuss issues as a bench of three and rely on clerk for legal issues
	Magistrates are criticised for inconsistency of sentencing for the same crimes in different local areas

Activities

1   Find out where your local Magistrates' Court is. How many court rooms does it have? Are its cases reported in your local paper? If so, cut out an article to show your class.

2   Who will hear these cases, where and why?

a   Amy is charged with murder. She is 19 years old. Also, would it be any different if she were 17 years old?

b   Barney has been summoned for a minor motoring offence.

c   Charlie has been charged with theft and he wants the trial to be over quickly.

Learning summary

You should now be able to:

know that magistrates are volunteers from all walks of life

know that they hear the vast majority of criminal trials and some minor family cases and they also sentence those convicted

know that they sit in benches of three.

Solicitors and barristers

Unlike most other countries, in the UK the legal profession is divided into two main branches: solicitors and barristers. Some argue that this is a better system, as each is able to specialise in their field – solicitors mainly advise clients and complete the necessary paperwork, and barristers mostly act as advocates in court and give objective opinion on legal issues. However, a single, fused profession works well in most other countries, where the lawyers decide for themselves which areas to specialise in and have a common system of training. This reduces costs and makes for better communication. Since solicitors and barristers tend to specialise in specific areas of work, their training, following a law degree, is different.

Role of solicitors

There are over 100,000 solicitors practising in the UK, with most forming partnerships and specialising in specific areas of work, e.g. **conveyancing**, commercial, criminal and family work.

Solicitors are the main providers of legal advice. Clients approach them directly, and often a legal problem is solved through interview, advice, letter-writing and negotiation. For those that are not, solicitors carry out the litigation process, preparing court documents, interviewing witnesses, corresponding on behalf of the client and instructing a barrister, if required.

Solicitors have full rights of audience to act as **advocates** in all courts, although they must demonstrate competence through further training in advocacy, and become a solicitor-advocate, to act in the Crown Court and above. A solicitor's responsibility is to their client and they enter a contractual relationship with them, so can sue a client for non-payment of fees and be sued by them for negligence.

Role of barristers

There are approximately 12,000 barristers, who act as self-employed legal professionals, although many others are employed by companies or public bodies as 'in-house' **counsel**, meaning they work in the legal department of the organisation but do not act as advocates in court.

Barristers who practise as advocates in court are not allowed to form partnerships and so must work alone but usually share **chambers** and a clerk. These barristers have **rights of audience** in all the UK courts, representing clients in civil and criminal trials.

Barristers' work usually comes to them from solicitors and clients are not usually allowed to contact barristers directly (called **direct access**). Since 2004, the public can access barristers who are specially trained in public access, in limited areas of work, not including litigation procedure. Organisations such as firms of accountants can instruct barristers directly through the licensed access scheme.

Objectives

In this topic you will learn:

how to describe and evaluate the training and role of solicitors and barristers

how to compare and contrast the training and role of solicitors and barristers.

○○ links

See page 25 to learn about negotiation.

For further information about working as a barrister, go to: www.barcouncil.org.uk/about/whatbarristersdo

Key terms

Conveyancing: buying and selling land.

Advocate: someone who represents a client in court.

Counsel: the name by which barristers are known.

Chambers (barristers): offices, facilities and clerks shared by a group of barristers.

Rights of audience: the authority to represent clients in court.

ILEX fellows: a fellow of ILEX is a legal executive. They must be aged over 25 and pass Parts 1 and 2 of the ILEX exams and have been working in 'qualifying employment' for five years.

Training of barristers and solicitors

A

Training of solicitors	Training of barristers
The **academic stage** is completed in one of three ways: 1. Completing a qualifying law degree (which covers core legal subjects) 2. Completing a degree in another subject then the Common Professional Exam/Graduate Diploma in Law 3. Becoming an **ILEX fellow** (of the Institute of Legal Executives)	The **academic** stage is completed in one of three ways: 1. Completing a qualifying law degree (Class 2:2 or above) 2. Completing a degree in another subject then the Common Professional Exam/Graduate Diploma in Law 3. Exceptional candidates without a degree may be accepted by the Bar Council
The prospective solicitor must then become a student member of the **Solicitors Regulation Authority**	The prospective barrister must then become a member of an **Inn of Court**: Grays, Lincoln, Inner Temple or Middle Temple. These provide support, training and resources for their members
The **vocational stage** of training begins with a one-year **Legal Practise course**, learning the practical skills required for the profession.	The **vocational stage** of training begins with a one-year **Bar Vocational Course**, learning the practical skills required for the profession. During this, they must complete 12 qualifying units through attending training, seminars, and dining events. On successful completion, they are "**called to the Bar**" (and can be called a barrister), but cannot practise as an advocate at this stage. Many work in legal departments of companies rather than practising in court
Next they must find a two-year **training contract** with an authorised training organisation (usually a firm of solicitors). ILEX fellows are exempt. During this, the **Professional Skills Course** must be completed.	The next stage is to find a one-year **pupillage** with an authorised training organisation (usually barristers' chambers). In the second six months they are able to take on their own cases
The solicitor is then fully qualified and is admitted to the **Roll of Solicitors**, usually working in a partnership with other solicitors. If they wish to represent clients in the Crown court or above they must undertake further training to become a solicitor-advocate.	The barrister is then fully qualified and is able to represent clients in all courts. They must work alone but usually share chambers

B *Legal professionals*

Activity

1. Look at the training chart.
   a. Who takes longer to qualify – a solicitor or barrister?
   b. Taking into account their role (work), why do you think this might be?

Apart from advocacy, their other main role is to give **counsel's opinion** (legal advice) to solicitors. They are able to be objective in assessing a case as they have not been involved with the client, as solicitors have.

Barristers operate under the **cab rank** rule, which means that they are obliged (as are taxis, hence the name!) to take the next case which is presented to them. This avoids them 'cherry-picking' only the best cases, leaving some defendants with no legal representation.

A barrister's responsibility is to the court and they are prevented from forming a contractual relationship with their clients and so cannot sue them for non-payment. They operate a blacklist system for solicitors who do not pay the barristers' fees.

Since the case of *Hall* v *Simons* (2000), barristers, like solicitors, may be sued for negligent work, both in and out of court.

Queen's Counsel

Experienced barristers and solicitor-advocates may apply to become Queen's Counsel (QC), which is awarded by an independent body, based on merit, and can be revoked if necessary.

C *Two professions or one?*

Arguments for a divided legal profession as in the UK (barristers and solicitors)	Arguments for a single profession as in the US (lawyers)
Each can specialise in their main areas – barristers specialise in advocacy and solicitors in giving advice to clients and drafting legal documents	Training is the same and so law students do not have to decide at an early stage which type of work they want to do when they qualify
A barrister can give objective advice on a legal problem as they have never met the client so is not personally involved and is able to judge the issues purely on the basis of the evidence presented	There is no breakdown in communications, or duplication of work or fees, as the same person could deal with a case right from the initial client interview through to representing them in court
The 'cab rank' rule for barristers means that a person should always be able to find somebody to represent them in court	A client is likely to feel more confident if they have dealt with the same person throughout their case rather than meeting the barrister on the day of the trial, as is often the case

AQA *Examiner's tip*

Don't forget that any question asking for a 'difference' requires consideration of both sides. For example, a difference between barristers and solicitors is that solicitors can advise clients directly in all cases whereas a barrister only has direct access in limited types of case.

Activities

2 Consider the arguments for and against having a legal profession with two different branches. Can you think of any points not mentioned? Which system, in your opinion, is better, and why?

3 Find out if other countries in the world have a divided legal profession like the UK.

4 Go to the Law Society and the Bar Council websites for further information on how each branch of the profession works.

Learning summary

You should now be able to:

explain the training of solicitors and barristers

describe the roles each of these carry out and to compare and contrast them

state arguments for and against a divided legal profession.

Judges

Title of judges

Objectives

In this topic you will learn:

how to name the judges in the UK courts

how to outline the role of judges in civil, criminal and appeal cases.

House of Lords

(set to become The Supreme Court late 2009)
Title of judges: Lords of Appeal in Ordinary (Law Lords)
Head: Lord Chief Justice
Role of judges: 5–12 Law Lords hear appeals on points of law from the
Court of Appeal (CA) or High Court (by **leapfrogging** CA)

Court of Appeal

Title: Lords Justices of Appeal (LJ)

Head of Civil Division: Master of the Rolls   Head of Criminal Division: Lord Chief Justice
Role: Civil appeals from High/County Court   Role: Criminal appeals from Crown Court

Cases are usually heard by a bench of three LJs

High Court

Title: Puisne judges (High Court judges)
The work of the High Court is divided into three divisions:

Queen's Bench Division	*Family Division*	*Chancery Division*
Head: Lord Chief Justice	Head: President of Family Dvn	Head: Chancellor of the High Court
Role: To hear complex or high value cases in Patents Contract, Tort, Commercial, Admiralty	Role: Family cases	Role: Equity, trusts, probate, tax, bankruptcy, companies

Each division of the High Court can also hear appeals from the courts below. These are called Divisional Courts

QBD	*Family*	*Chancery*
Divisional Court: supervises and rules on legality of decisions of public bodies and lower courts	Divisional Court: appeals from Magistrates' Court – family proceedings	Divisional Court: appeals from County Court on bankruptcy/land

County Court	**Crown Court**
Title: Circuit judges and District judges	Title: High Court judges, circuit judges and **Recorders**
Role: Hear undefended divorce and most civil cases of lower value/complexity	Role: Trial of serious crimes
Keep order, rule on law, decide outcome, and also decide remedy if liable	Keep order, rule on law, sum up to jury, sentence offenders
	Also hears appeals based on fact and sentencing and committals for sentencing from Magistrates' Court

Magistrates' Court

In place of a bench of magistrates, District judges sit in larger towns, hearing minor crimes

 UK courts and judges

Title of judge	Name of court	Cases heard	Role: Keeping order	Role: Ruling on points of law	Role: Deciding the verdict or outcome	Role: Deciding the sentence or remedy
District judge (magistrates' court)	Magistrates'	Criminal Summary and either-way offences		✓	✓	(same sentencing powers as lay magistrates)
District judge	County	Civil Small claims cases and some fast-track cases	✓	✓	✓	✓
Recorders	Crown	Criminal Either-way and indictable offences	✓	✓	✗ (verdict decided by a jury)	(can sentence up to the maximum for the offence)
Circuit judge	County	Civil Fast-track and some multi-track cases	✓	✓	✓	✓
Circuit judge	Crown	Criminal Indictable offences	✓	✓	✗ (verdict decided by a jury)	(can sentence up to the maximum for the offence)
High Court judge	Crown	Criminal The most serious indictable offences, e.g. murder trials	✓	✓	✗ (verdict decided by a jury)	(can sentence up to the maximum for the offence)
High Court judge	High	Civil The most complex or high-value civil cases (multi-track)	✓	✓	✓	✓
Lords Justices of Appeal	Court of Appeal	Civil and criminal Appeal cases from the courts below	✓	✓	May uphold or reverse the lower court's decision (civil), uphold or quash a conviction (criminal), or order a re-trial	May change the sentence (criminal), or change the remedy (civil), if appropriate
Lords of Appeal in Ordinary	House of Lords	Civil and criminal	Public do not attend – no need to keep order	✓	Their rulings on the law may mean that the original verdict is changed	Appeals on a point of law only – therefore do not generally rule on sentence or remedy

Under the Constitutional Reform Act 2005, the Judicial Appointments Commission has been responsible for appointing judges from 2006. The Lord Chancellor, a government minister, is no longer the head of the judiciary, which is now the Lord Chief Justice. The new Supreme Court, due to open in late 2009, will be separate from the Houses of Parliament, so the Law Lords will not be part of the House of Lords.

The role of a judge

Depending on the court the judge sits in, his/her role will vary (see the chart opposite).

F *A judge*

Did you know ??????

One of the Law Lords is actually a Law Lady! And three of the Court of Appeal judges are Lady Justices of Appeal.

Key terms

Leapfrogging: when the Court of Appeal is 'missed out', and the appeal is taken to the House of Lords directly from the High Court, as the House of Lords made the law that is the subject of the appeal.

Recorder: an experienced barrister or solicitor-advocate who works as a part-time judge for 15–30 days per year.

Activity

5 Decide which court and which judge/s would preside over/decide the trial in the following cases:

a David wishes to sue a store which has refused to refund his money on a faulty kettle.

b Emily was found guilty of a minor offence and wishes to appeal against the sentence, which she feels is too severe.

c Freddie's barrister thinks the judge at his original trial in the Crown Court misapplied the law and wishes to appeal.

⃝⃝ links

See Chapters 2 and 3 to remind yurself of the work of civil and criminal courts.

Also: to find out more about what judges do; the clothes they wear; how much they earn, go to: **www.judiciary.gov.uk**

Learning summary

You should now be able to:

know which judges sit in which courts

know the type of work each judge will do, depending on the court and the case heard.

4

You should now:

✔ know how magistrates and juries are selected

✔ know the work magistrates and juries perform

✔ know how solicitors and barristers are trained

✔ know the work solicitors and barristers carry out

✔ know the titles of the judges and the areas of work carried out in the UK courts.

Revision questions

1 What are the three qualifications of a juror?

2 Which Acts govern the selection process for a jury?

3 Who is disqualified from jury service?

4 Which courts and types of case may juries sit in?

5 What is the jury's role?

6 What are the main criticisms of juries?

7 Why is jury trial a popular method of trying cases?

8 How are magistrates selected?

9 What qualifies a person to apply to be a magistrate?

10 What do magistrates do in the criminal justice system, including administrative tasks?

11 What do magistrates do in the civil justice system?

12 What are the main advantages of having magistrates?

13 What are the main criticisms of using magistrates?

14 How are the roles of juries and magistrates similar?

15 How are the roles of juries and magistrates different?

16 Not including training, name two differences between the roles of solicitors and barristers.

17 Describe how a solicitor is trained.

18 Describe how a barrister is trained.

19 What is meant by a QC, and how are these appointments made?

20 What are the major differences between a magistrate and a District Judge (Magistrates' Court)?

21 Discuss the arguments for and against a divided legal profession.

22 Who is the head of the judiciary?

23 What roles does a Magistrates' Court legal advisor carry out?

24 What is a Youth Court?

25 What is a Family Proceedings Court?

26 How do magistrates decide on an appropriate sentence?

27 What is a majority verdict and when may it be accepted and what is a unanimous verdict?

28 What is the correct title of the Law Lords?

29 Which court do Lords Justices of Appeal sit in?

30 Which two courts may a High Court judge sit in, and to hear what types of case?

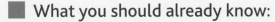

5   Sources of English law

■ What you should already know:

✔ the structure of courts operating in England and Wales (Chapter 1)

✔ the titles of and roles undertaken by judges (Chapter 4).

■ Chapter contents

■ Introduction to sources of English law

Law is made by a variety of persons or bodies, and may take different forms. The law of England and Wales takes the following main forms:

■ legislation (Acts of Parliament)

■ case law

■ European Union law (EU law).

Together, these are said to be the laws of England and Wales.

Legislation is law made by Parliament, and is the highest (supreme) form of law passed within England and Wales. When law is being passed by Parliament it is known as a Bill. Once the Bill has been passed, it is known as an Act of Parliament or Statute. There are different types of Bill that are passed by Parliament. We are most concerned with Public Bills, of which there are two types, i.e. Bills, which are sponsored by the Government, and others which are sponsored by individual Members of Parliament (Private Members Bills).

Case law (or the common law) is judge-made law. The judges have a number of roles to play in creating and developing law, such as interpreting legislation passed by Parliament. They therefore add to the existing law in terms of judgments which set precedents. In addition, many areas of law have been created by judges making rules in cases which appear before them. Collectively, these judge-made laws are known as case law.

European Union (EU) law is the highest-ranking form of law and takes precedence over all the others. If the European Union passes a new law, or changes an existing law, then English law must follow. If English law is different to EU law, then English law must change.

Legislation

■ The legislative process

Every **Act of Parliament** must follow a set procedure through both Houses of Parliament and beyond. If this procedure is not followed or completed then the Bill cannot become law. The procedure is as follows.

Ideas and discussion

Ideas come from a variety of sources, the most obvious of which is the Government. Bills can also come from other sources, e.g. individual Members of Parliament and law reform agencies such as the Law Commission.

A Government Bill may start out with a **Green Paper**, which is a statement of Government intent inviting discussion, comment and criticism from interested parties. This is usually followed by a **White Paper**, which contains firm Government proposals.

Drafting

Bills are drafted by specialist barristers known as Parliamentary Counsel to the Treasury. Drafting is a highly specialised skill involving detailed technical language which judges, in court, are eventually going to have to interpret.

A *The House of Commons*

First reading

The first **reading** is the formal presentation of the Bill to Parliament (usually the House of Commons first) and MPs will have an opportunity to read the Bill.

Second reading

This follows about two weeks later. The Bill will be debated in the Commons (general principles only). Following the debate there is a Division (vote). Assuming the Bill is carried, it will pass to the next stage.

Committee stage

A small committee of about 18 MPs will meet to discuss the Bill in detail. Changes can be made at this stage. These are known as **amendments**.

Report stage/third reading (House of Commons)

This is a final debate in the Commons on the Bill and any amendments followed by a final vote.

House of Lords

The whole process is repeated in the Lords. Their Lordships can put amendments to the Bill and can even block its progress altogether for up to a year. As a result of the Parliament Acts 1911 and 1949 the Commons has the final say on all Lords amendments.

Royal Assent

Nowadays **Royal Assent** is a formality, but the Queen (or someone acting on her behalf) must sign the Bill before it can become an Act of Parliament.

Publication

All Acts must be published through Her Majesty's Stationery Office.

> **AQA Examiner's tip**
>
> Accurately learn the process of Parliament passing an Act. This is a common examination question. Discuss both the advantages and disadvantages of this process. Commentary questions should always look at both sides of the argument and finish with a conclusion.

> **Remember**
>
> That both the House of Commons and House of Lords, and the Queen have to approve a Bill before it becomes an Act of Parliament.

■ Advantages and disadvantages of parliamentary law-making

B *Parliamentary law-making*

Advantages	Disadvantages
The House of Commons is elected by the people, so Parliamentary law-making is a democratic process	The whole process of passing an Act, from initial ideas to Royal Assent is very slow and can take years. The Act could be out-of-date before it is even passed
Parliament controls what legislation it passes, so the Act can be passed when it is needed and will cover exactly what Parliament intends to legislate on	The judges have to apply the new Act in court, and how they interpret the Act can mean that the original intention of Parliament can be lost
The process of passing an Act is lengthy and detailed and great care is taken when the Bill is drafted and when it is being considered by both Houses of Parliament	Parliament is a political body, and too much time and effort is spent on politics and not enough on law-making

> **Activity**
>
> **Parliamentary Bills**
>
> Log on to the Parliamentary website using the links on this page. Follow the link to see which Bills are currently being discussed in Parliament. Choose one Bill and make a list of the main changes the Bill will make to the law. Discuss in class whether these changes are good or not.

∞ **links**

The Houses of Parliament website: **www.parliament.uk**

Her Majesty's Stationery Office website: **www.opsi.gov.uk**

> **Learning summary**
>
> You should now be able to:
>
> describe accurately the process of passing an Act of Parliament
>
> discuss the advantages and disadvantages of the Parliamentary law-making process.

> **Did you know** ???????
>
> That Parliament only sits for about seven months a year and only has the time to pass, at most, about 60 Acts of Parliament a year?

Case law or common law

There are over 500,000 reported cases in English law, each of which lays down a rule or rules of law. Collectively, these rules are known as case law or the common law.

Cases are vital in areas where Parliament has not legislated, e.g. tort and contract. Even where Parliament has legislated, e.g. theft, case law is still important for interpreting the meaning of the Act.

The 'backbone' of the common law is known as the doctrine of **precedent**, i.e. the rule which states that each case lays down a rule(s) of law which **may** or **must** be followed in later cases involving the same point of law, irrespective of the facts. This is sometimes known as *stare decisis* (the standing of decisions).

The doctrine of precedent relies on two key things:

The system of law reporting

Nowadays all cases heard in the superior courts are officially reported and appear within various editions of law reports, e.g. the All England Law Reports, the Weekly Law Reports. In addition, some newspapers regularly print law reports, e.g. *The Times*, *The Guardian*, *The Independent*. Law reports can also be found on online databases, e.g. Lawtel, LexisNexis.

The hierarchy of the courts

Judgments in higher courts, such as the House of Lords, have always commanded the greatest respect. The rule is that the decisions of higher courts are binding on lower courts, i.e. lower courts must follow the rule of law (precedent) set by the higher court. The order of the hierarchy is as follows:

A *The hierarchy of the courts*

The House of Lords	Binds all lower courts. Not bound by its own previous decisions (since the 1966 Practice Statement)
Court of Appeal	Bound by the House of Lords. Binds all lower courts The Civil Division is generally bound by its own previous decisions The Criminal Division is not so strictly bound
High Court	Bound by all the appeal courts above. Binds the inferior courts below High Court Judges do not have to follow each other's decisions
Crown Court	Bound by the appeal courts above. Binds the inferior courts below, in particular the Magistrates' Court. Own decisions? – probably depends on the status of the judge
Inferior courts (Magistrates, Youth, County, Tribunals etc.)	Bound by all above Bind no-one, including themselves

Having heard a case argued before him, the judge(s) must pass judgment. It is from the judgment that the precedent is drawn. However, not all the judgment is relevant in determining the precedent. Later judges will only be looking for one specific part of that earlier judgment. Take a look at the Structure of a judgment box on page 46.

The precedent in a case is based on the *ratio decidendi*, and it is this part of the judgment which **may** or **must** be followed in later cases.

Other matters which the judge comments upon (*obiter dicta*) cannot form binding precedents even if the comment comes from a Law Lord. However, *obiter dicta* statements can form persuasive precedents.

Binding and persuasive precedents

A binding precedent is one which a judge **must** follow. This does not mean that he must follow the **decision**, but he must follow the *ratio decidendi*. The *ratio decidendi* will be binding, depending in which court the previous case was decided. This can be seen in the hierarchy of courts table.

A persuasive precedent is one which the judge does not have to follow, but one which he **may** choose to follow. There are various ways of creating persuasive precedents including judgments made by lower courts, *obiter dicta*, statements and decisions of the Judicial Committee or the Privy Council such as *The Wagon Mound* (1967) (see page 56).

Advantages and disadvantages of judicial precedent

Key authority – precedent

In the 1966 Practice Statement, Lord Gardiner, on behalf of the Law Lords, said the following:

'Their Lordships regard the use of precedent as an **indispensable foundation** upon which to decide what is the law and its application to individual cases. It provides at least some degree of **certainty** … Their Lordships nevertheless recognise that **too rigid adherence** to precedent may lead to **injustice** and **restrict the proper development of the law**. They propose therefore to modify their present practice and while treating former decisions of this House as **normally binding**, to **depart from a previous decision** where it appears **right** to do so … This announcement is not intended to affect the use of precedent elsewhere than in this House.'

B *Advantages and disadvantages of judicial precedent*

Advantages	Disadvantages
Certainty Once a precedent has been set in the appeal courts, this will lay down a rule of law which will then be applied in similar fact situations. Thus it is possible to predict, with a fair degree of certainty, what the decision would be in a current dispute and therefore whether it is worth taking or defending the action	**Inflexibility** Once a precedent has become established, it becomes very difficult to change, especially where society has moved on. Thus the precedent can become out-of-date
Possibility of growth Existing rules can be added to and new rules created by decisions in the courts without the need for Parliament to pass a new Act	**Illogical distinction between cases** A judge who does not like a previous binding precedent will often point to some minor difference in the facts (this is called distinguishing between cases) so that he can avoid having to follow that precedent. He may feel he has done justice in his case, but often he will leave the law in a confused and uncertain state
Practical nature of the rules Obviously cases are from real life, whereas Acts of Parliament are only theoretical	**Bulk and complexity** There are over 1,000 volumes of official English Law Reports, containing over 500,000 cases, with the precedents 'hidden' within each case. This can be regarded as both cumbersome and difficult to both find and learn
Detail It would be impossible for Parliament to replace all the detailed rules contained in cases by legislation	

Learning summary

You should now be able to:

describe the main features of the doctrine of precedent

discuss the advantages and disadvantages of judge-made law.

5.3 The relationship between the different sources of law, including EU law

To understand the relationships between the different sources of English Law, you first need to know something about the law of the European Union.

■ European union (EU) law

A completely new source of law was created when Parliament passed the European Communities Act 1972 and the United Kingdom joined the Common Market (now the European Union) on 1 January 1973.

As a result of the Act, all English courts are bound to recognise and apply EU law, wherever it comes from. There are different forms of EU legislation.

Regulations

Regulations apply to all member states and are immediately binding in English law without any need for Parliament to do anything.

Key case

Re Tachographs: EC Commission v UK (1979)

The UK Government did not implement a regulation that tachographs should be installed in all vehicles used for carrying goods. Instead the Government left it to the road haulage industry to introduce the regulation on a voluntary basis. The matter went before the European Court of Justice, which decided that:

- the regulation provided that member states must adopt the law; and
- regulations are immediately binding on member states.

Directives

Directives bind all member states, but action needs to be taken to give the directive the force of law. In the UK this is normally done by statutory instrument. A statutory instrument is a law made by a government minister, with the approval of Parliament.

European law has also had an important effect on the courts where an issue of European law is raised in a case. Lower courts have discretion (can choose) whether or not to refer the case to the European Court of Justice in Luxembourg for a ruling. The House of Lords has very little such discretion; it usually must refer the case to Luxembourg. Such rulings are then binding on English law and judges must follow them.

■ The relationship between the different sources of law

Parliamentary supremacy

The constitutional theory is that Parliament can make any law it chooses and in that sense is supreme (there is **Parliamentary**

Objectives

In this topic you will learn:

how to demonstrate an outline understanding of EU law and the main forms it can take

how to demonstrate an outline understanding of Parliamentary supremacy and the impact that other sources of law have upon Parliament.

Key terms

Regulations and directives: different forms of EU law.

Parliamentary supremacy (source of law): the principle that, under English law, Parliament is the highest law-making body.

⚭ links

For basic information about the European Union, see:
www.europa.eu

AQA Examiner's tip

Make sure you understand the difference between a regulation and a directive.

You may also be expected, in examination questions, to discuss the relationship between Parliament and the EU and also Parliament and the courts.

Did you know ??????

That there are 27 countries in the EU, with a combined population of 493 million.

supremacy). People who try to challenge the authority of an Act of Parliament before a court are unlikely to succeed as can be seen in the *Cheney* v *Conn* (1968) case.

The European Union

However, in practice, there are a number of restrictions on the power of Parliament.

In cases of conflict between English law and European law, EU law prevails. This was settled in the *Factortame* cases (1990–2000).

It can be argued that if the UK were to leave the EU, we could take back the powers we have given to the EU. This is legally true, but economically and politically very unlikely.

The courts

The judges accept that their job is to carry out the will of Parliament, and that an Act of Parliament is the supreme source of law. However:

1. it is the courts' job to interpret the Act, and how this is done is up to individual judges;

2. there are large areas of law not governed by statute (the common law), where Parliament has not made the rules, so the judges must. Parliament retains the right to pass a new Act to change an area of the common law which Parliament does not like.

Human rights

The Human Rights Act 1998 came into effect in October 2000. Since that time, any new Act of Parliament must contain a statement that it complies (or fails to comply) with the European Convention on Human Rights. In practice, the vast majority of Acts will comply and this somewhat restricts the power of Parliament. The ability to ignore the Convention, which Parliament still has, would only rarely be exercised.

> **Key case**
>
> ### *Cheney* v *Conn* (1968)
>
> The claimant objected to his tax assessment on the ground that the Government was using some of his tax to make nuclear weapons. His objection was that this was illegal under the Geneva Convention.
>
> The Court applied the Finance Act 1964 (under which his tax had been assessed) in preference to the Convention which had been accepted by Parliament in 1957 (the later Act prevails). The judge commented, 'It is not for the court to say that an Act of Parliament, **the highest law in this country**, is illegal'.

∞ links

See Topic 9.3 for more information on human rights.

> **Remember**
>
> Parliament is supreme in English law terms, but EU law takes priority over English law.

> **Key case**
>
> ### *Factortame Ltd* v *Secretary of State for Transport (No 2)* (1991)
>
> The issue in this case was the Merchant Shipping Act 1988, which provided that 75% of shareholders in companies operating fishing boats in UK waters had to be British. Spain argued that this was contrary to the Treaty of Rome. It would take two years to get a ruling. Spanish boat owners asked the English courts to suspend the 1988 Act until the issue had been decided. The House of Lords referred the matter to the European Court of Justice which decided that EU law must take priority over domestic (national) law, even where there only **may** be a conflict.
>
> The case was referred back to the House of Lords, which was obliged to suspend the relevant part of the 1988 Act.
>
> The importance of *Factortame* (1991) is thus that it shows that, if the British Parliament passes a new law which arguably conflicts with European law, the British courts have power *in some circumstances* to grant a temporary injunction to prevent the UK authorities from enforcing that UK law while the matter is being sorted out.

> **Activity**
>
>
>
> a. Log on to the EU website listed in the link on page 48. Find and write down 12 key facts about the European Union. Share these facts with your classmates.
>
> b. Discuss in class whether EU law should take priority over English law.

> **Learning summary**
>
> You should now be able to:
>
> describe the main forms of EU law
>
> discuss the relationships between Parliament and both the EU and the courts.

5

You should now:

✔ know how Parliament passes an Act of Parliament

✔ know how the system of precedent operates in the courts and therefore how the common law develops

✔ know what is meant by Parliamentary supremacy

✔ know how the supremacy of Parliament is affected by European Union law and by the role of the judges in the development of case law

✔ know how to critically analyse law-making procedures including the key advantages and disadvantages of both law-making by Parliament and the courts.

Revision questions

1 Identify the two Houses of Parliament.

2 What is the difference between a Green and White Paper?

3 Who drafts most Bills which eventually go through Parliament?

4 What is the main difference between a First and Second Reading?

5 What is the purpose of the Committee stage?

6 What are the powers of the House of Lords with a Bill that their Lordships do not want to pass?

7 What is the importance of the Parliament Acts?

8 What is the name of the process which changes a Bill to an Act of Parliament?

9 Who publishes all Acts of Parliament?

10 Identify two advantages and two disadvantages of the process of Parliamentary law-making.

11 What is another name for case law?

12 What is meant by a precedent?

13 Identify and explain the importance of law reports.

14 In precedent terms, what is the highest court in the English legal system?

15 Which Appeal Court must generally follow its own previous decisions?

16 Which Appeal Courts have the ability to overrule their own previous decisions?

17 Briefly explain what is meant by the terms 'ratio decidendi' and 'obiter dicta'.

18 What is the key difference between a binding and a persuasive precedent?

19 Identify three different examples of persuasive precedents.

20 Identify two advantages and two disadvantages of the system of judicial precedent.

21 In terms of precedent, what important speech was made in 1966 in the House of Lords and who made it?

22 When did the United Kingdom join the Common Market (European Union) and as a result of which Act of Parliament?

23 What is the key difference between a European regulation and directive?

24 What would be the difference if a point of EU law was raised in the House of Lords as opposed to the Court of Appeal?

25 What was confirmed in the case of *Cheney* v *Conn* (1968)?

26 What was confirmed in the *Factortame* cases (1990–2000)?

27 Briefly explain how judges can ignore the will of Parliament, despite the supremacy rule.

28 Briefly explain how the Human Rights Act 1998 can restrict the power of Parliament.

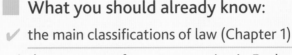

6 The law of tort

Key case

Christie v Davey (1893)

Christie, a music teacher, used her home for lessons, musical evenings, etc. Davey, her neighbour, was fed up with the noise. He retaliated by knocking on the wall, beating on tin trays, whistling and shrieking. Christie sued Davey in the tort of private nuisance. The court decided that both Christie and Davey were being a nuisance, but because Davey had acted maliciously he was liable. An injunction was granted to restrain Davey's actions.

What you should already know:

✔ the main classifications of law (Chapter 1)

✔ the structure of courts operating in England and Wales (Chapter 2)

✔ remedies (Chapter 3).

Chapter contents

Introduction to the law of tort

The word 'tort' is French for 'wrong'. In law, a tort is a **civil** wrong committed by one individual against another. Liability arises because the defendant is in breach of a duty fixed by law and the claimant will, as a result, be entitled to a remedy, often damages.

Differences between a tort and a crime

A tort is a wrong committed against an individual, e.g. negligence, trespass etc., whereas a crime is an offence committed against the State, e.g. murder, theft etc.

Damage and liability

This distinction is very important, and students often mix up these two terms.

Damage is what the claimant suffers, e.g. personal injury.

Damages are financial compensation for that suffering (provided the defendant is liable).

To win a tort case, the claimant has to prove that he has suffered damage. However, some torts are **actionable** *per se* (in themselves): i.e. the claimant only has to prove that the tort occurred; he does not have to prove that he has suffered damage. The best example is the tort of trespass.

Malice

The word malice implies motive. In the crimal law, the accused's mental state is crucial in deciding his criminal liability. In the law of tort, the defendant's motive is usually **irrelevant**, except in some torts, especially the tort of **nuisance**. This is illustrated in *Christie* v *Davey* (1893).

Negligence

Duty of care

Negligence is the most common, and therefore the most important of all the torts. For the claimant to succeed in a negligence case, he will have to prove the following:

- that the defendant owed the claimant a **duty of care**
- that the defendant was in breach of that duty of care
- that as a result of this breach, the claimant suffered damage.

The rule relating to duty of care was established in the most famous case in legal history.

Donoghue v *Stevenson* (1932)

A lady bought a bottle of ginger beer for Donoghue, her friend, in a café. The bottle was made of dark glass. She poured some out for her friend who drank it, and she then poured the rest of the ginger beer into her friend's glass. Along with the ginger beer, out came the decomposed remains of a snail. Donoghue suffered gastric illness and nervous shock. Donoghue sued Stevenson, the manufacturer of the bottle of ginger beer.

It was decided (by Lord Atkin in the House of Lords), that because the manufacturer owed a duty of care to anyone who could be affected by their actions (their neighbours), the company did owe a duty of care to Mrs Donoghue and therefore her claim could succeed.

Lord Atkin was effectively saying that, whatever we are doing we must be careful not to harm those around us (our **neighbours**), who we can reasonably foresee could be affected by what we do. More recent cases, in particular *Caparo* v *Dickman* (1990), have refined the neighbour principle. Modern law requires not only **foreseeability**, but also that the individuals are reasonably **proximate** (close) and that it is **just, fair and reasonable** to impose a duty of care. The following cases illustrate.

Bourhill v *Young* (1943)

Bourhill, a pregnant Scottish fishwife, got off a bus. Young, a motorcyclist, drove negligently past the bus and collided with a car 15 yards away. Young was killed. Bourhill heard the collision and later saw blood on the road. She suffered nervous shock and subsequently miscarried. Bourhill sued Young's estate for negligence. The court decided that Bourhill's claim should fail because she was not owed a duty of care. In modern terms, a court may well say that she was not immediately proximate to the accident and that it would not be fair to impose a duty of care for the benefit of every pedestrian who witnesses an accident.

In this topic you will learn:

how to describe and apply the law of negligence

how to describe and apply the law of occupiers' liability for both visitors and trespassers

how to describe and apply the principle of vicarious liability

how to discuss critically the law on negligence and related topics.

⚭ links

A link to a video interview with Lord Denning and a teaching video on *Donoghue* v *Stevenson* (1932): **www.thepaisleysnail.com**

Duty of care: a duty owed by the defendant.

A neighbour: a person who can be affected by the defendant's actions.

Foreseeability: what the defendant should predict could happen.

Proximity: how 'close' the defendant and claimant are, physically or emotionally.

Just, fair and reasonable: the defendant will only be liable if that is a fair outcome.

Try to remember the key cases which show how the legal principles work, e.g. the neighbour principle comes from *Donoghue* v *Stevenson* (1932). Briefly describe the facts, the decision and the principle. Don't worry about the date.

Alcock v *Chief Constable of South Yorkshire Police* (1991)

At Hillsborough football ground, 95 spectators lost their lives and over 400 were injured when supporters tried to cram into one end of the stadium. Alcock, in the other end of the stadium, saw the accident in which his brother-in-law was killed. Alcock suffered nervous shock and sued the police who admitted they had been negligent, but argued that Alcock's injury was not reasonably foreseeable.

The House of Lords, at the same time as this case, considered nine other claims from persons either witnessing or watching television pictures of the accident in which their relatives were either killed or injured. It was decided that it would not be just, fair and reasonable to impose a duty of care on the police in respect of the claimant who was at the other end of the ground and not able to see, in detail, what was happening to his brother-in-law.

McLoughlin v *O'Brian* (1983)

McLoughlin was a wife and mother at home. Two miles away, her husband and three children were involved in a serious car accident caused by O'Brian. McLoughlin was told about the accident and visited her family in hospital immediately afterwards. She suffered nervous shock, sued O'Brian for negligence and her claim succeeded because it was foreseeable that she would suffer harm. In modern terms, it would be irrelevant that she was not physically close (though she was in terms of relationship) and it was just, fair and reasonable that she should be owed a duty of care.

> **Remember**
>
> In law, a person is only a 'neighbour' if any loss they may suffer is foreseeable, the two people are proximate and the court considers it 'just, fair and reasonable' to impose a duty of care.

Activity

1. In a series of other cases arising out of the Hillsborough disaster, the courts had to consider whether the following claims could be brought against the police. Look at the list of claimants:

   - those who witnessed the deaths first hand and at close range
   - close family
   - more distant family
   - relatives who identified the bodies some hours later
   - those who watched on TV or listened on the radio
   - rescuers such as the stewards on duty at the ground
   - the police who were on duty in the ground.

   a Which of these claimants were owed a duty of care and which were not?

   You will find the answers at:
   www.stbrn.ac.uk/other/depts/law/newnotes/notes41.htm

   b How fair were these decisions? Discuss in class which of the cases you think should have been decided differently.

> **Did you know** ??????
>
> That a negligence claim in the High Court involving serious personal injuries can take years to get to court and will certainly cost tens of thousands of pounds in legal costs.

> **Learning summary**
>
> You should now be able to:
>
> describe the neighbour principle and how the claimant proves that he was owed a duty of care
>
> apply this law, using the relevant cases.

Breach of the duty of care

The defendant's conduct is measured against the conduct of a **reasonable man** placed in the defendant's position. If the defendant's conduct falls below the reasonable man standard, he will be in **breach of the duty of care**. If his conduct is above that standard, he is not negligent.

When judging this standard, the courts have to balance various risk factors. These risk factors are as follows:

- the **risk** involved in the defendant's conduct
- the **likelihood** of damage/injury occurring
- the **potential consequences** of that damage/injury
- the **means** by which the risk could be eliminated completely
- the fact that the risk may be **justified** in the public interest.

How these factors apply can be seen in various Key cases.

Res ipsa loquitur (the facts speak for themselves)

In the vast majority of negligence cases, it is the claimant who has to prove that the defendant was in breach of a duty of care. In some cases, negligence by someone is so **obvious** that the burden of proof reverses so that the defendant has to prove that he was not in breach, and therefore not negligent. In such cases, the facts speak for themselves (*res ipsa loquitur*). In most such cases, the claimant's action will succeed, unless the defendant can show that the fault lies elsewhere and not with him. The following cases illustrate.

Key case

Paris v Stepney Borough Council (1951)

Paris was a mechanic employed by Stepney BC. Stepney BC knew that Paris had one good eye. Paris was not issued with safety goggles, because other workers did not need them. One day, a piece of metal went into his eye and blinded him. Paris sued Stepney BC for negligence.

It was decided that engineering is clearly a high-risk activity which carries a high likelihood of serious injury which could have been easily avoided by supplying Paris with safety goggles. Not surprisingly, the council were found to be in breach of their duty of care and the claim succeeded.

A *Goggles must be worn*

Key case

Bolton v Stone (1951)

A cricket field was near a public highway. During the previous 35 years only about half-a-dozen cricket balls had ever cleared the field and the fence, and no one had ever been hit until Bolton, who was standing on a road outside the ground, was struck. She sued the cricket club for negligence.

The court decided that, in the circumstances, this was not a particularly risky activity and it was very unlikely that a passer-by would suffer any injury. Clearly also, the public benefited from playing and watching the cricket. Therefore, the club had acted reasonably and were not in breach, and therefore the claim failed.

B *'Howzat!'*

Key case

Grant v Australian Knitting Mills (1936)

Grant bought some 'long-johns' made by Australian Knitting Mills (AKM) who had used a chemical during manufacturing, which had not been removed. Grant contracted dermatitis which spread from his ankles upwards. Grant sued AKM for negligence.

It was decided that it was very obvious that someone had breached a duty of care. Therefore the *res ipsa loquitur* rule applied, and it was then up to the defendant to prove that no negligence had occurred, which could not be done on the facts. Therefore the claim succeeded.

Key case

Pearson v NW Gas Board (1968)

A gas explosion killed Pearson's husband and destroyed her home. The court applied the rule *res ipsa loquitur* but NW Gas Board (NWGB) showed that severe frost caused the gas leak and there was no reasonable way in which the explosion could have been prevented.

The court decided that this looked like an obvious case of negligence where the *res ipsa loquitur* rule would apply. However, NWGB was able to prove that the exceptional weather had caused the explosion and therefore the claim failed.

Activity

2. In *Mullin v Richards* (1998), two 15-year-old girls were fighting with plastic rulers. One of the rulers broke and one of the girls was blinded in one eye by a fragment of plastic. The injured girl sued for negligence.

   Consider whether or not there has been a breach of duty of care by the girl who inflicted the injury. What factors do you think the court will take into account?

   When you have discussed the case with your classmates, you will find the court decision at:
   www.webjcli.ncl.ac.uk/1998/issue4/wenham4.html

AQA Examiner's tip

Breach of duty is a straightforward issue provided you can remember the reasonable man test and the five risk factors.

Res ipsa loquitur applies in exceptional cases where negligence is obvious and the claimant no longer has to prove breach.

Learning summary

You should now be able to:

describe how a breach of the duty of care is proved and also the exception of *res ipsa loquitur*

apply this law, using the relevant cases.

Damages

There must be some damage, often physical injury or damage to property, suffered by the claimant. A person cannot successfully sue for negligence if he has not suffered damage.

The claimant may not be able to recover for all the losses he has suffered. Here we are concerned with the issue of **remoteness of damage**. This is the rule that the claimant cannot recover for damage unless:

- the defendant directly caused the damage and
- the defendant could foresee that his actions would cause that type of loss.

These tests can be seen in the following cases.

Key case

The Wagon Mound (1961)

Oil was negligently spilt from a ship and floated across Sydney harbour to a ship repairer where sparks ignited the oil and caused damage to a wharf and a ship. The ship owners were sued for negligence.

It was decided that although the fire was a direct result of the spillage, it could not be foreseen that floating oil would normally catch fire in these circumstances. Therefore, the ship owners were not liable for negligence.

C *A modern view of Sydney Harbour*

This Australian case was decided by the Judicial Committee of the Privy Council. While it is not strictly binding on English law, it is regarded as being highly persuasive (see Chapter 5). Three years later, the following English case came before the Court of Appeal:

Key case

Doughty v Turner Manufacturing (1964)

Doughty was injured in an explosion in an iron foundry caused by a careless employee. An explosion had never happened before but on occasions employees had been injured by splashes of hot metal. Doughty sued Turner Manufacturing for negligence.

The court decided that although injury by **splashing** was foreseeable, injury caused by **explosion** was not. Therefore, the company was not liable for Doughty's injuries.

What do you think would happen if a similar explosion took place later and an injured employee sued his employer for damages?

If you think the answer is that he would probably win because the explosion would now be foreseeable, you are probably right! Do you think this is fair on the first injured employee?

3 In *Smith* v *Leech Brain* (1961), Smith was splashed by molten metal through his employer's negligence and he suffered a burn on his lip. The burn aggravated a pre-existing cancerous condition and he died. His widow sued for negligence.

Consider whether the employer should be liable for the burn suffered by Smith or should be liable for his death by cancer.

When you have discussed the case with your classmates, you will find the court decision at: **www.sixthformlaw.info**. You can use the search function to find this case.

Vicarious liability

As you have just read in *Doughty* v *Turner Manufacturing* (1964), when a person is injured by the actions of an employee, it is the employer who is sued rather than the employee. We will develop this topic in Chapter 9, but it is useful that you should understand how this rule operates in the context of a negligence case.

Providing the employee is acting within the **course of his employment**, the employer will be responsible for any loss incurred as a result of the employee's actions. This principle is known as **vicarious liability**. *Limpus* v *London General Omnibus Co* (1862) case illustrates how this principle works.

This principle of vicarious liability will be further discussed in Chapter 9.

Contributory negligence

Contributory negligence is where the claimant is at least in part responsible for the damage he has suffered. An example would be a negligent driver running someone over where that person had stepped into the road without looking.

Before 1945, contributory negligence was a complete defence for the defendant, but this rule was thought to be unfair on the claimant. Under the Law Reform (Contributory Negligence) Act 1945, the claimant is still awarded damages, but his damages are reduced by the percentage he has contributed to his loss. *Sayers* v *Harlow UDC* (1958) case illustrates how the law works in this area.

4 In *Froom* v *Butcher* (1975), a motorist was injured in a road accident. The accident was the fault of the other driver, but the claimant was not wearing a seat belt, which at the time was recommended but not legally required. The motorist sued for negligence.

Do you think the motorist should receive full damages or reduced damages? Would the legal position be exactly the same today?

When you have discussed the case, the answers can be found at: **www.sixthformlaw.info**. You can use the search function to find this case.

Limpus v London General Omnibus Co (1862)

A bus driver racing to a stop to collect passengers, against company rules, deliberately obstructed the driver of a bus belonging to a rival company, overturning the latter vehicle, and injuring Limpus, a passenger. Limpus sued LGO in the tort of negligence.

It was decided that even though the bus driver was ignoring company instructions, he was still driving the bus which was what he was employed to do, i.e. he was doing his job. Therefore, the employer was liable for Limpus's injury.

Sayers v Harlow UDC (1958)

Sayers got locked in a public toilet owned by Harlow UDC, due to a defective door. She was injured when trying to use the toilet roll holder to climb out. Sayers successfully sued Harlow UDC for negligence, as it had not properly maintained the door, but reduced Sayers's damages by 25% because she contributed to her own downfall by standing on the toilet roll holder.

Learning summary

You should now be able to:

describe when an employer will be liable for the actions of an employee

apply this law, using the relevant cases

describe the relevant law on damage in negligence cases

apply this law, using the relevant cases

describe and apply the law on contributory negligence, quoting a relevant case in support.

Occupiers' liability

This area of law is generally regarded as a part of the law of negligence and concerns the liability of **occupiers** of premises for injury caused to people, either **visitors** or **trespassers** who are on another's land.

Occupiers' Liability Act 1957

Under the Act, a **common duty of care** is owed to all lawful visitors to land/premises, e.g. postman, employee, invited guest, cinemagoer etc.

Under the Act, the occupier owes to all visitors **the duty to take such care as is necessary to see that the visitor will be reasonably safe in using the premises for the purpose for which he is entitled to be there**.

Possible defences which an occupier could plead include:

- that the injury was caused by the fault of a competent **independent contractor**
- that the visitor consented to the risk of injury
- that the visitor was partly responsible for his injury (contributory negligence), which may reduce the damages.

Key terms

Visitor: a person lawfully on another's land.

Trespasser: someone unlawfully on another's land.

Independent contractor: a person who has control over their own actions at work.

Prescriptive right: a right acquired over time.

Allurement: an attraction which tempts someone onto another's land.

Key case

AC Billings and Son Ltd v Riden (1958)

AC Billings and Son Ltd (ACB), building contractors, left the entrance to a house in a dangerous condition. Riden, a lawful visitor, left the house after dark, fell and suffered injury. Riden sued ACB, and the claim succeeded.

Key case

Cotton v Derbyshire Dales DC (1994)

The District Council owned a path which was close to an **obviously** dangerous cliff, and had not put up a warning notice. The court decided that a landowner is not required to warn visitors of obvious dangers. Cotton's claim failed.

D *No sign to warn of danger*

Occupiers' Liability Act 1984

This Act is concerned principally with the duties owed to trespassers on another's land, or those people using a right of way across another's land.

The nature of the duty can be summarised as a duty of common humanity whereby the occupier, through warnings/notices must take reasonable steps to offer the non-visitor some degree of protection from dangers the occupier is aware of.

For example, the farmer who keeps a bull in his field where there is a right of way must, at least, put up a notice warning people of the danger.

Child trespassers

The duty owed to children is set at a much higher standard than it would be to an adult. The rules can be summarised as follows:

- An occupier must be prepared for children to be less careful than adults.

- What may be a warning to an adult may not be so to a child.

- Children can more easily acquire a **prescriptive right** to trespass, effectively turning them into visitors.

- Children can be **allured** into trespassing by something attractive on the occupier's land.

- Very young children should be in the charge of a competent adult.

E *Trespassers will be prosecuted*

> ### Key case
>
> ### *Cook* v *Midland GW Railway of Ireland* (1909)
>
> Midland kept a turntable on their land near a public road. To the Railway Company's knowledge, children habitually came onto the land and played with the turntable. Nothing was done to stop them. A child aged four was injured on the turntable.
>
> The court decided that even though the child was very young, the railway was an **allurement** and the children had also acquired a **prescriptive right** to trespass, effectively making them visitors. The railway company was liable for negligence.

> ### Activity
>
> 5. In *British Railways Board* v *Herrington* (1972), a child trespasser was electrocuted and severely injured on British Railways Board (BRB)'s land. The fence guarding the line was broken. BRB knew that children had been seen trespassing on the railway in that area, but had done nothing about it. An action was brought on behalf of the boy, Herrington, who was aged six at the time of the incident.
>
> a What factors do you think the House of Lords would have taken into account before arriving at a decision in this case?
>
> b Why do you think this might have been a difficult decision for the House to decide?
>
> c What decision do you think the House of Lords eventually made?
>
> d Discuss your findings with your classmates and see if you arrived at the same conclusions.
>
> Afterwards, you can find the decision in the case at: **www.safetyphoto.co.uk**

> ### Key case
>
> ### *Phipps* v *Rochester Corporation* (1955)
>
> A boy aged five, accompanied by his sister aged seven, fell into a hole and broke his leg. Rochester Corporation was responsible for the hole, and was sued on the boy's behalf.
>
> It was decided that a landowner is entitled to expect that a young child should be supervised by a competent adult, not by a seven-year-old. Phipps's claim failed.

> ### AQA Examiner's tip
>
> Students often fail to distinguish between the two different Occupiers' Liability Acts. The 1957 Act applies to visitors; the 1984 Act generally to trespassers. Occupiers owe a greater duty to visitors.

> ### Learning summary
>
> You should now be able to:
>
> describe the liability of occupiers of land for injuries caused to visitors, trespassers and child trespassers on their land
>
> apply this law, using the relevant cases.

There are two different types of nuisance: **public** and **private**.

Public nuisance

Public nuisance is defined as 'an unlawful act or omission which endangers or interferes with the lives, safety or comfort of the public generally or some section of the public', e.g. a noisy factory which affects the whole neighbourhood.

Public nuisance is both a crime and a tort and both can be brought by the Attorney-General.

Private individuals can also sue in public nuisance provided they can prove they have suffered particular damage over and above that suffered by everyone else.

Objectives

In this topic you will learn:

how to describe the law relating to nuisance, both public and private

how to apply the law of nuisance and draw appropriate conclusions

how to demonstrate an outline critical awareness of the law of nuisance.

Key case

Castle v St Augustine's Links (1922)

A golf club had a hole just next to a public road. Golf balls were frequently hit onto the road. One day, Castle, a taxi driver, lost an eye when he was struck by a golf ball. Castle sued the club for public nuisance. The court decided that the golf balls were a potential danger to all road users (and therefore a public nuisance), but Castle had suffered more than anyone else, therefore he was entitled to damages for public nuisance.

Key case

R v Shorrock (1993)

Shorrock let a field on his farm, not knowing that it was to be used for an 'acid house' party attended by 3,000 people. There was massive local disruption. Shorrock was prosecuted for public nuisance, and found guilty.

Private nuisance

Private nuisance is defined as 'an unlawful interference with a man's use of his property or with his health, comfort or convenience', e.g. noisy neighbours.

The following issues, depending on the facts, may be relevant to private nuisance.

Health and comfort

The claimant needs to prove that he was prevented from enjoying his property.

Locality

What amounts to a nuisance will vary from area to area.

Extra sensitivity

The claimant cannot take advantage of the fact that either he or his property is particularly sensitive.

Utility of the nuisance

Chip shops, factories etc. are all useful things. However, their usefulness does not give them the right to be a nuisance to their neighbours.

Repetition

A private nuisance must be more than just a one-off occasion.

Key case

A-G v PYA Quarries (1957)

PYA operated a quarry at which blasting took place. Stones and splinters were hurled out of the quarry and the dust and vibration caused discomfort to the residents of a nearby housing estate. The Attorney-General sued for an injunction, which was granted to limit the activities at the quarry.

BLASTING SCHEDULED
TRAFFIC DELAYS POSSIBLE

DAY   DATE   TIME

A *Beware – low flying rocks*

links

A Government department website dealing with noise nuisance is: **www.defra.gov.uk/environment/noise/suffer/suffer4.htm**

Malice

Making a noise unintentionally can amount to a nuisance. Making a noise deliberately or spitefully (maliciously) will amount to a nuisance.

Prescriptive rights

A prescriptive right to do something, e.g. commit a nuisance, is something that may be acquired over a period of time. For a nuisance, the law normally recognises a period of about 20 years.

Defences

There are a number of defences which may be pleaded in private nuisance cases:

- statutory authority, e.g. planning permission from the local authority may permit your neighbour to carry out building work on his house
- triviality, e.g. a bonfire on 5 November would be too trivial to take to court
- lawful use of land: in *Bradford Corporation* v *Pickles* (1895), it was held that a person who uses his land lawfully does not commit a nuisance
- the defendant could try and plead that the claimant came to the nuisance or that he has tried to stop the nuisance. However, neither would be valid defences.

Remedies

The claimant can apply for an injunction, i.e. to stop or reduce the nuisance, and/or sue for damages. The claimant can also try and deal with the nuisance himself. This is called abatement, but is not generally recommended!

The following cases illustrate these principles on nuisance.

Robinson v Kilvert (1889)

Kilvert manufactured paper boxes in the cellar of a house and leased the floor above to Robinson. Kilvert heated the cellar with hot, dry air. This raised the temperature of Robinson's premises, used for storing very sensitive paper. Because of the heat, Robinson's paper was ruined. Robinson sued Kilvert for private nuisance, but his claim failed. He could not take advantage of the extra sensitivity of his property.

Hollywood Silver Fox Farm v Emmet (1936)

Because of a dispute over a sign, Emmet deliberately caused a shotgun to be fired near Hollywood Silver Fox Farm (HSFF)'s land. The noise disrupted the breeding of HSFF's silver foxes. HSFF sued for private nuisance and succeeded, particularly because Emmet had acted maliciously.

Bliss v Hall (1839)

Hall had been a candle-maker for three years before Bliss moved next door. Bliss immediately complained about the smell and sued for private nuisance. Bliss's claim succeeded. It was irrelevant that he had moved to the nuisance. (See also *Christie* v *Davey* (1893) on page 51.)

Key terms

Public nuisance: affects a large group of people.

Private nuisance: interferes with an individual's right to enjoy their property.

Activity

There are various alternatives to suing someone in nuisance. As you have seen, the Attorney-General can take action on behalf of local residents. Alternatively, the victim can complain to the local council or Environmental Health Department. In extreme cases, an individual can bring a case directly to the Magistrates' Court.

Consider why these alternatives may provide a better option than taking civil action in the courts. Ask around your friends, relatives and classmates. Has anyone else been the victim of a nuisance, and how was it resolved?

AQA Examiner's tip

Understanding the difference between public and private nuisance is the key to scoring well in nuisance questions in exams. The examiner will often have both types in the same question.

Remember

That a claimant in private nuisance must own or occupy land which is affected by the nuisance. A claimant in public nuisance need not.

Learning summary

You should now be able to:

describe, using cases, and apply, the law on nuisance

discuss whether suing for nuisance is the only or best way of dealing with this problem.

Trespass

Trespass to the person

In the law of tort, there are three different forms of trespass to the person, namely false imprisonment, **assault** and **battery**.

False imprisonment

False imprisonment is defined as the infliction of bodily restraint on another without lawful justification, e.g. a wrongful arrest or a kidnapping.

False imprisonment does not mean that the claimant is actually locked up (though he often will be). Merely being made to stay in one place unlawfully and against his will and with no means of escape would be false imprisonment. The following cases illustrate these principles.

Bird v Jones (1845)

A bridge company lawfully closed a public footpath over Hammersmith Bridge. Bird, a pedestrian, insisted on using the path. However, he was prevented from going any further by two policemen, who barred his way. Bird was told of an alternative route but he refused to go that way. Bird sued in the tort of false imprisonment, but his claim failed. He was not prevented from using an alternative route and therefore had not been imprisoned, falsely or otherwise.

John Lewis and Co Ltd v Tims (1952)

Tims and her daughter were detained for almost an hour (according to them) by a store detective on suspicion of shoplifting, before a senior manager decided that the police should be called.

It was decided that following a citizen's arrest, the police must be called within a reasonable time. On the facts, the store had not acted unreasonably and therefore Tims' claim failed.

Meering v Grahame-White Aviation Co (1919)

The claimant was brought to his employer's office to be questioned about a theft of some paint. Although the claimant did not know, his exit from the office was blocked by two security guards. When the claimant found out, he brought an action for false imprisonment and his claim succeeded. His not knowing that he had been detained was irrelevant because trespass is **actionable** *per se*.

Assault

An assault is defined as an attempt or threat to apply unlawful force to the person of another whereby that person is put in fear of immediate violence.

The threat of violence according to the definition must be immediate.

For example, A is on a train leaving the station. B is on the platform. A shakes his fist at B and threatens to beat him up. At least in theory, this should not be an assault because the threat cannot be immediate.

Key terms

Assault: an attempt or threat to apply force.

Battery: the application of force.

Actionable *per se*: trespass does not require proof of damage by the claimant.

Key case

R v Ireland (1998)

This case involved a series of silent telephone calls sent by the defendant to three female victims. They suffered mental injury and the defendant was convicted of actual bodily harm.

N.B. This is clearly a criminal case, but the same principles would apply to the tort of assault.

Although there used to be some doubt, current law seems to suggest that words on their own can constitute an assault. What is not in doubt is that words can negate an assault as in *Turberville* v *Savage* (1669).

Battery

Battery is defined as the intentional application of unlawful force, however slight, to the person of another, against their will. Examples would include a punch or a push or even a kiss where it was not welcome.

There are several defences that the defendant can plead in an assault/battery case. These include: self-defence; that it was an accident, e.g. in a crowded train; that the claimant consented, e.g. in a boxing ring; that a householder was using reasonable force to eject a trespasser; or that a parent was only inflicting reasonable chastisement (smacking) on a child.

Turberville v *Savage* (1669)

Key case

Savage placed his hand on his sword and said 'If it were not assize time, I would not take such words from thee' (translated meaning 'If the judge weren't in town, I would attack you'). Turberville sued Savage for assault, but the claim failed. By his words, Savage made it clear that he was not going to attack Turberville.

Nash v *Sheen* (1953)

Key cases

Nash asked her hairdresser, Sheen, for a perm but a tone rinse was applied instead. The court decided that this did amount to a trespass because the hairdresser acted outside of the permission granted by the customer.

Harrison v *Duke of Rutland* (1893)

Harrison was crossing the Duke's land on a public footpath. He saw that the Duke and his friends were bird shooting so he started waving his arms around and shouting, hoping to scare the birds away. The Duke ordered Harrison's removal and Harrison was injured by a servant in the process. Harrison sued in the tort of trespass to recover damages.

The court decided that Harrison became a trespasser when he used the path unlawfully. The Duke was therefore entitled, using reasonable force, to have him removed. Harrison's claim failed.

∞ links

A useful local authority document on the torts of nuisance and trespass can be found on: **www.bridgend.gov.uk**

▨ Trespass to land

Trespass to land is defined as the interference with the possession of land of another without lawful justification.

Note that possession is not the same as ownership, i.e. the tort can be committed against a tenant, and not just the owner. For example, if a landlord entered property without permission, his tenant could sue him for trespass to land.

Forms of trespass to land

The law recognises three different forms of trespass to land:

1 **entry** on the land of another
2 **remaining** on the land of another
3 **placing objects** on the land of another.

Harrison v *Duke of Rutland* (1893)

Key case

We have already examined the facts of this case. From a trespass to land point of view, Harrison was entitled to be on the Duke's footpath, but became a trespasser from the moment he left the path and/or started behaving unreasonably.

Entry on the land of another

Entry is the most common form of trespass to land, and will still be a trespass even if done in complete ignorance, e.g. crossing an unmarked boundary.

A person does not trespass on land where he is entitled to be, e.g. in a shop, library, pub, college, etc. However, permission to enter is usually limited to a lawful specified activity, e.g. shopping, reading, drinking, studying etc. However if someone abuses his right of entry, for example, by stealing books in a library, he will almost certainly be a trespasser.

Remaining on the land of another

This will only be a trespass where the person had a right of entry originally (and therefore did not trespass originally), but refuses to leave when asked to do so, i.e. he outstays his welcome. An example would be refusing to leave the pub at closing time.

Placing objects on the land of another

Placing objects on the land of another is known as continuing trespass because the objects remain until removed, giving the claimant a fresh right of action each day the objects remain on his land. A good example would be fly-tipping (dumping waste on someone's land).

Note that a person's possession of land extends both above and beneath its surface. A good example of this would be a neighbour's tree which overhangs the garden next-door – this amounts to a trespass.

Defences to trespass to land

There are various potential defences which can be pleaded in relation to this tort. These include:

Entry by lawful authority

This would include a policeman entering your house with a search warrant.

An accidental/unintentional entry

A good example would be someone who was pushed, or a stray parachutist!

Entry to abate a nuisance in an emergency

A good example would be a fireman breaking in to put out a fire.

Express or implied permission granted by the person in possession

The obvious example would be inviting someone for a meal, or the postman delivering the mail.

Key case

Amory v *Delamirie* (1722)

A chimney-sweep's boy found a jewel and handed it in to a jeweller, Delamirie, for valuation. Delamirie refused to return it. Amory sued Delamirie in the tort of conversion, and the boy's action succeeded. As the person who found the jewel, he had the right to possession. Only the owner has a better right and the jeweller was not the owner. Therefore, the boy was entitled to the return of the jewel.

AQA Examiner's tip

Make sure you understand the following distinctions:
assault and battery;
trespass to goods and **conversion;** trespass to land and private nuisance.
Confusing these legal terms is a common mistake in examinations.

Key case

Ballet v *Mingay* (1943)

The defendant borrowed an amplifier from the claimant. He then lent them to a third party. Mingay sued Ballet in the tort of conversion.

The court decided that the action should succeed. A loan contract requires that the goods loaned are returned to the rightful owner at the end of the loan period or on request. As the goods had been lent to another, he could no longer return the goods as required. Therefore he had committed the tort of conversion.

The differences between private nuisance and trespass to land

Both of these torts are connected to land. It would be useful to remind you of the differences between them.

A

Trespass to land	Private nuisance
Actionable *per se*	Some damage must be proved
Direct physical interference with land	Indirect interference with land
Requires unlawful entry by person/thing	No entry on land required
Single act will suffice	Must be repeated
Can only be a tort	Private nuisance can only be a tort. Public nuisance is both a tort and a crime

Kirk v *Gregory* (1876)

A storeowner moved some jewellery to a different shop. From there it was stolen. The owner of the jewellery sued the storeowner for trespass to goods.

It was decided that the storeowner had moved the property without authorisation. Therefore, the owner's action for trespass to goods succeeded.

Trespass to goods

Trespass to goods is defined as the intentional or negligent interference with the possession of goods of another.

This whole area of the law is now governed by Act of Parliament – Torts (Interference with Goods) Act 1977. Wrongful interference with goods now takes two different forms:

- tort of conversion
- trespass to goods.

Tort of conversion

There are four ways in which tort of conversion may be committed:

Remember

The tort of trespass in all its forms is actionable *per se*. Therefore the claimant does not need to prove that he has suffered damage.

B *Tort of conversion*

How tort of conversion may be committed	Examples
By taking	Theft
By detention	Keeping goods which belong to another, such as a library book. See *Amory* v *Delamirie* (1722)
By wrongful delivery	Giving something away which belongs to another. See *Ballet* v *Mingay* (1943)
By complete destruction	Smashing a window

C *Trespass to goods*

How tort of trespass to goods may be committed	Examples
By damaging the goods	Returning a torn library book
By moving the goods	See *Kirk* v *Gregory* (1876)

Activity

a   Collect the cuttings from your local newspaper with the reports of a range of criminal cases. Re-arrange these cuttings, not as crimes, but as potential tort cases. You should be able to find many of the torts that have been discussed in this chapter and you might be quite surprised how many criminal cases could also give rise to actions in tort.

b   Compare your cuttings with your classmates. Have you managed to find every single version of all the torts in this chapter?

Learning summary

You should now be able to:

describe and apply the law on trespass to the person, trespass to land and trespass to goods

discuss the differences between the torts of trespass and nuisance.

Defences and remedies

General defences in tort

A defence is something the defendant may plead in order to escape liability. A general defence is one that can be pleaded for a number of different torts. There are several such defences.

A *General defences in tort*

Defences	Torts
Volenti non fit injuria (consent)	No injury can be caused to a willing person, i.e. a person who consents. Thus if the claimant consents to whatever has happened to him, he cannot later sue the defendant for any injury or loss suffered See *Hall v Brooklands Auto Racing Club* (1933)
Necessity	This defence can be pleaded where, for example, the defendant commits a tort to prevent something worse happening See *Cope v Sharpe* (1912)
Inevitable accident	This defence covers damage or injury which was beyond the defendant's control See *Stanley v Powell* (1891)
Statutory authority	Where an Act of Parliament or local by-law authorises what would otherwise be a tort, no action will lie against the defendant. For example, council road-works which block your drive would not be a nuisance
Act of God	This defence covers an act of nature which could not have reasonably been foreseen See *Nichols v Marsland* (1876)

Objectives

In this topic you will learn:

how to describe in outline and apply the general defences that can be pleaded in tort cases

how to demonstrate an outline understanding of the major remedies available in tort cases.

⚭ links

A summary of the amounts of injury damages in tort cases:
www.lawrencehamblin.com/cms/catsection/pi_jsb_guidelines_summary.html

Key terms

Volenti non fit injuria: the defence of consent.

Necessity: committing a tort to prevent something worse.

Act of God: an act of nature which could not have been foreseen.

Injunction: an order to stop doing something.

Key cases

Hall v Brooklands Auto Racing Club (1933)

Hall paid for admission to Brooklands to watch the racing. During the race, a car shot over the barrier after a collision and killed Hall. An accident like this had never happened before. Hall's widow sued the Club for negligence, but her claim failed. Not only was there no

B

breach (because the Club had not acted unreasonably), but also Hall had consented to the risk when he paid to go and watch the racing.

Cope v Sharpe (1912)

Fire broke out on the claimant's land. The gamekeeper from next-door went onto the claimant's land and set fire to a strip of land to prevent the fire spreading and harming livestock. The claimant sued for trespass to land, but the claim failed. The gamekeeper had 'trespassed' because of a clearly perceived necessity and therefore his actions were justified.

Key case

Stanley v Powell (1891)

On a shooting party, the claimant was injured when a pellet from the defendant's gun struck a tree, ricocheted and hit him. The court decided that there was no liability. This was a genuine accident.

C

Nichols v *Marsland* (1876)

A rainstorm caused the defendant's artificial lake to overflow, damaging the claimant's land. The court decided that there was no liability for something beyond the defendant's control.

D

Remedies in tort

There are a number of remedies which can be applied for in a tort case, but the following two are the most important.

Damages

The most common legal remedy sought by the victim of a tort is an action for damages. Damages are designed to compensate the claimant, i.e. to put him in the he would have been in had the damage not occurred. According to Lord Denning in *Jefford* v *Gee* (1970), the claimant can be compensated for:

- special damages – provable damage such as car repairs
- loss of future earnings – what the claimant cannot earn in the future
- pain and suffering – depending on the nature of the injury
- loss of amenity – the inability to enjoy a sport or hobby
- the injury itself – according to a published tariff depending on the extent of the injury.

Injunction

This is a remedy which prevents the defendant from committing the tort again in the future. Good examples would be nuisance or a trespass to land.

Chadwick v *British Railways Board* (1967)

A rescuer, who voluntarily spent some 12 hours helping to deal with the casualties at the wreckage following a particularly harrowing train crash, suffered foreseeable psychiatric injury. He was awarded general damages of £600 (in addition to £900 for lost wages as special damages) against British Railways, whose negligence had led to the crash.

A-G v *PYA Quarries* (1957)

The facts of this case you will find in the section on public nuisance. You should remember that the Attorney-General chose to sue for an injunction, which was granted to limit the activities at the quarry.

> **Activity**
>
> Have a look at the table of damages at www.lawrencehamblin.com/cms/catsection/pi_jsb_guidelines_summary.html
>
> Make a note of the key types of injury and the level of damages awarded.
>
> Do you agree with the levels of damages awarded, or do you think some awards are too high or too low? Compare your views with those of your classmates looking at the same table.

> **Did you know** ? ? ? ? ? ?
>
> In 2006/7, the National Health Service dealt with well over 10,000 negligence claims by patients and paid out over £600,000,000 in damages.

> **Learning summary**
>
> You should now be able to:
>
> describe in outline and apply the major defences pleaded in tort cases
>
> describe in outline and apply the major remedies in tort cases.

> **AQA Examiner's tip**
>
> Many candidates have difficulty in applying both the defences and remedies in tort cases. Make sure you understand the key elements of the defences and also when different remedies are applied for.

Chapter summary

6

You should now:

✔ understand in outline, the general principles of the law of tort and the differences between tort and crime

✔ understand the tort of negligence, including occupiers' liability and vicarious liability

✔ understand the torts of private and public nuisance

✔ understand the torts of trespass to the person, goods and land

✔ understand in outline the general defences which can be pleaded in a tort case

✔ understand in outline the major remedies in tort cases

✔ understand in outline some of the key issues relating to the law of tort.

Revision questions

1. What does the word 'tort' mean?

2. What is the key difference between liability in tort and crime?

3. What is meant by 'actionable *per se*'?

4. What is meant by 'malice' in the law of tort?

5. According to Lord Atkin, who is a 'neighbour'?

6. What are the three tests for determining whether someone is owed a duty of care?

7. Identify the five risk factors used to determine a breach of duty of care.

8. What is meant by '*res ipsa loquitur*', and what is the effect of this principle?

9. Identify the two tests which are used to decide whether or not damage is or is not too remote.

10. What is meant by the 'thin skull' rule?

11. What is meant by 'vicarious liability'?

12. What is the effect of contributory negligence in a negligence case?

13. What is the difference between a visitor and a trespasser?

14. What is the difference in terms of the level of duty owed by an occupier to a visitor and a trespasser?

15. In relation to child trespassers, what is an allurement and what is a prescriptive right?

16. What are the key differences between public and private nuisance?

17. What does an individual have to prove to be able to sue in public nuisance?

18. Identify five of the factors a court may consider in a private nuisance case.

19. Identify two alternative courses of action rather than suing someone in private nuisance.

20. Identify the three forms of trespass to the person.

21. How long can someone be held before calling the police following a citizen's arrest?

22. What is the difference between assault and battery?

23. Identify three ways in which a person can commit trespass to land.

24. Identify two defences to trespass to land.

25. Identify four differences between trespass to land and private nuisance.

26. Identify three ways in which someone can commit conversion and two ways in which they can commit trespass to goods.

27. Identify four of the general defences in tort.

28. Identify the two major remedies available in tort cases.

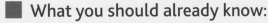

7 Criminal law

In this chapter you will learn:

how to demonstrate an outline understanding of the principles of criminal liability

how to demonstrate an understanding of the definition and key elements of fatal offences, non-fatal offences and property offences

how to demonstrate an outline understanding of the general defences to crime.

■ What you should already know:

✔ crimes are offences deemed to be against the State (Chapter 1)

✔ criminal trials are held in Magistrates' Courts and the Crown Court (Chapter 2)

✔ magistrates, district judges (Magistrates' Court) and juries decide the verdict in criminal trials (Chapter 2, Chapter 4)

✔ the 'burden of proof' in criminal cases is 'beyond reasonable doubt' (Chapter 1).

■ Chapter contents

Elements of criminal liability

Actus reus   *Mens rea*   Strict liability

Fatal offences

Murder
Manslaughter
- Voluntary – Diminished responsibility; Provocation
- Involuntary – Constructive (unlawful act); Gross negligence

Non-fatal offences

Common assault – assault and battery
Assault occasioning ABH
Unlawful, malicious wounding or infliction of GBH

Property offences

Theft   Robbery   Burglary   Making off without payment

General defences

Insanity   Automatism   Intoxication
Duress (by threats)   Duress of circumstances/necessity
Self-defence   Consent

■ Introduction to criminal law

In this chapter you will learn about the elements of criminal liability. You will learn the differences between murder and manslaughter. You will learn about the major non-fatal offences and about offences against property. You will study the defences which may be raised in a criminal trial. Finally, you will learn how to apply these principles to examination-style questions.

Elements of criminal liability

For a defendant to be found guilty of a crime, the prosecution must prove that the person carried out all the elements of the offence they have been charged with. For most crimes, the definition of the offence will contain elements of what the defendant must have *done* (or in some cases, *didn't do*) and elements of what the defendant must have been *thinking*, to be guilty of that crime. Unless the prosecution can prove both, then the defendant is not guilty.

■ Actus reus

The part of a definition which concerns the *doing* or the outward part of the crime is called the *actus reus*, which is Latin for 'guilty act'.

A person will only be criminally liable for a *failure* to act (omission) if they were under a legal duty to act at the time, such as a parental duty, or an employment (contractual) duty, or a duty from an Act of Parliament (statutory duty).

For some crimes, the *actus reus* is to cause a certain *result*. For the crime of murder, for example, you will not commit the *actus reus* if your actions did not cause the person's death.

The thin skull rule

The thin skull rule means 'you take your victim as you find them', meaning that, if a more serious injury occurs than was intended, because of some condition of the victim, the defendant is still responsible for causing the full result of his actions. This applies equally to physical or mental conditions/beliefs.

■ Mens rea

The part of a definition which concerns the *thinking* or inward part of the crime is called the *mens rea*, which is Latin for 'guilty mind'.

The *mens rea* for many crimes requires an *intent* to do something, for example the *mens rea* for murder is intent to kill or cause serious harm. A **direct intent** to do something means you set out to do it. It was your aim or purpose. Intention is not the same thing as motive or desire. Intent is what you *meant* to do and motive is *why* you wanted to do it. Indirect intent is where you knew this would virtually certainly happen, even if you did not specifically *want* it to.

Another common type of *mens rea* is **recklessness**. For example the crime of common assault – battery, for which the *mens rea* is either an intent or recklessness to use unlawful force.

In law, the word 'reckless' means that the defendant had foresight (was aware) of the risks but went ahead with his actions anyway.

Objectives

In this topic you will learn:

how to demonstrate an outline understanding of the elements of criminal liability (*actus reus* and *mens rea*)

how to demonstrate an outline understanding of the elements of strict liability offences.

Key cases

R v White (1910)

A man poisoned his mother's tea, intending to kill her. By chance, she died of an unrelated heart attack, before the poison could take effect. So, he wasn't guilty of her murder as he did not actually cause her death.

R v Blaue (1975)

A man stabbed a teenage girl and she refused a potentially life-saving blood transfusion because of her religious beliefs. He was still guilty of causing her death.

Key terms

Direct intent: your aim, purpose or desire.

Recklessness: foresight of a risk, but carrying on anyway.

Transferred malice

This principle means that *mens rea* towards an *intended* victim can be transferred to the *actual* victim. For example, if you intend to shoot one person, but he ducks and you actually shoot another, your intent to kill is transferred to the person you shot.

■ Strict liability

Strict liability crimes are an *exception* to the rule that both *actus reus* and *mens rea* must be proved to establish guilt, as they require proof of *actus reus* only. Parliament creates these crimes by passing an Act, which makes it clear that no *mens rea* is required. Often these crimes are either minor, regulatory offences, such as not displaying a valid car tax disc, where proving *mens rea* would be difficult, or an offence involving the safety of the public, where greater care is encouraged to avoid the offences, such as selling food unfit for human consumption.

Evaluation of strict liability

- It encourages greater care.
- *Mens rea* does not need to be proved for minor regulatory offences.
- However, a person may be guilty even if they are not really to blame.

> **Key cases**
>
> *Recklessness*
>
> ### R v Cunningham (1957)
>
> A man ripped out a coin-operated gas meter, to take the contents, but did not turn off the gas, which leaked into the next flat, injuring its elderly occupants. The House of Lords confirmed the meaning of recklessness in this case.
>
> ### R v Gemmell and Richards (2003)
>
> Boys aged 11 and 12 set fire to newspapers and put them into wheelie bins outside a supermarket. The fire spread, setting light to the building, causing £1 million damage. They were not reckless since it was accepted that they did not foresee the risk of the fire spreading in this way.

> **Key cases**
>
> *Strict liability*
>
> ### PSGB v Storkwain (1986)
>
> Mr Storkwain was a pharmacist who **unknowingly** dispensed prescription only drugs on the basis of a forged prescription. He was guilty of the offence of dispensing the drugs without a valid prescription, as the Medicines Act 1968 made it clear this is a strict liability offence.
>
> ### Meah v Roberts (1977)
>
> A restaurant manager's staff **unknowingly** sold lemonade which had been contaminated with caustic soda, left in the bottle when the pumps were cleaned. This was a strict liability offence under the Food and Drugs Act 1955.

> **Key case**
>
> ### R v Latimer (1886)
>
> A man struck out at an intended victim with a belt, but it bounced off and severely injured someone else. His intention to injure one person was transferred to his actual victim.

> **Activity**
>
> 1 From the definitions of the crimes below, pick out the *actus reus* (what the person has to have done/not done).
>
> a Theft: to dishonestly appropriate property belonging to another with the intention of permanently depriving the other of it.
>
> b Murder: the unlawful killing of a human being, under the Queen's Peace, with intent to kill or cause serious harm.

> **Learning summary**
>
> You should now be able to:
>
> demonstrate an understanding of the elements of criminal liability and strict liability crimes.

■ Murder

The legal definition of murder is 'the unlawful killing of a human being, under the Queen's peace, with malice aforethought, express or implied,' as stated by a judge named Sir Edward Coke, 400 years ago. Murder is a **common law** offence and so is not defined in an Act of Parliament.

Actus reus of murder

The *actus reus* of murder is to unlawfully cause a person's death. This is the same *actus reus* that is required for manslaughter. Certain killings are *lawful*, for example, in times of war or in self-defence. So the killing must have been *unlawful* and the defendant must be responsible for causing the death. As discussed previously, if it cannot be proved that the defendant's actions *caused* the death, then they do not have the *actus reus* of murder (See *R v White* (1910)).

Mens rea of murder

What separates the crimes of murder and manslaughter is the *mens rea* required. For murder, the *mens rea* is 'malice aforethought' which has a legal meaning: intent to kill or cause GBH (serious harm). Therefore, either an intent to kill (express malice) or an intent to cause GBH (implied malice), will be enough for a murder conviction, as confirmed in *R v Vickers* (1957).

If the jury finds a defendant guilty of murder, the **mandatory** sentence given by the judge is life imprisonment, although the judge will recommend a minimum term to be served before they may be considered for release on licence.

■ Manslaughter

There are two main types of manslaughter: voluntary and involuntary. A manslaughter conviction means that the judge may give a **discretionary** life sentence, but a lesser sentence is often given. Voluntary manslaughter is where, on a murder charge, a partial defence has been accepted. Involuntary manslaughter is where there was no intent to kill or cause serious injury.

Voluntary manslaughter

If charged with murder, a defendant may plead one of the partial defences to murder, found in the Homicide Act 1957: the two main defences are diminished responsibility and provocation.

Diminished responsibility: Homicide Act 1957 s 2

This defence to murder relies on evidence that, at the time of the killing, the defendant was:

- suffering from an 'abnormality of mind' resulting from a specific cause: either disease, injury, inherent cause or arrested mental development and
- this 'substantially impaired his mental responsibility' for the killing.

Objectives

In this topic you will learn:

how to demonstrate an understanding of the definition and key elements of murder

how to demonstrate an understanding of the definition and key elements of voluntary manslaughter (due to successfully pleading the partial defence of diminished responsibility or provocation on a charge of murder)

how to demonstrate an understanding of the definition and key elements of involuntary manslaughter (due to causing death through a dangerous criminal act or through gross negligence).

Key terms

Common law: judge-made, or case law.

Mandatory: compulsory; the judge has no choice, as opposed to discretionary sentences, where they do.

Discretionary: the judge has a choice.

Remember

If a person unlawfully kills, intending to cause either serious injury or death, then this is murder.

Diminished responsibility

R v Ahluwalia (1992)

After her husband threatened to burn her face with an iron on top of years of domestic abuse, the defendant threw caustic soda and petrol over him as he slept and set fire to it. He died six days later. On appeal it was accepted that she was suffering from diminished responsibility due to battered woman syndrome and severe depression. (A plea of provocation was rejected as she had not had a 'sudden' loss of control.)

R v Martin (2001)

The Norfolk farmer, Tony Martin, had been burgled several times. This had an even greater impact on him, as he suffered from depression and paranoia due to childhood abuse. He became paranoid that intruders would enter his home and developed unusual behaviour, sleeping fully-clothed on top of his bed, with a shotgun. He allowed his house to become derelict around him, boarding up all his windows, as a fortress. On the night in question, he shot a 16-year-old burglar in the back, killing him as he was trying to escape through a window. The case caused heated debate on the issue of self-defence, which was rejected in his case, as he used 'excessive force'. He was originally convicted of murder, and this was reduced on appeal to voluntary manslaughter on the grounds that his paranoid personality disorder amounted to an 'abnormality of mind' for the purposes of diminished responsibility. His life sentence was reduced to five years imprisonment, of which he served three years.

> **Remember**
>
> A defendant cannot be *charged* with voluntary manslaughter, as this is the result of successfully raising a partial defence under the Homicide Act 1957 to a charge of murder.

The three elements of diminished responsibility have been explained by the courts as follows:

1 Abnormality of mind

In *R v Byrne* (1960) it was confirmed that an abnormality of mind is: 'a state of mind so different from that of ordinary human beings that a reasonable man would term it abnormal.' This means the jury will decide from the evidence whether they consider the defendant's mind to have been abnormal at the time of the killing.

Examples of abnormalities of mind include:

- battered woman syndrome and severe depression: *R v Ahluwalia* (1992)
- post-natal depression and PMT: *R v Reynolds* (1988)
- irresistible impulses of a sexual psychopath: *R v Byrne* (1960)
- paranoid personality disorder: *R v Martin* (2001)
- severe depression leading to a 'mercy killing': *R v Price* (1971).

2 From a specific cause

The abnormality of mind must be caused by one of these four things:

- disease – of the body or brain, such as brain tumour
- injury – e.g. blow to head
- inherent cause – not necessarily from birth – includes all forms of mental illness that are not due to disease or injury but doesn't include being intoxicated by drink or drugs
- arrested mental development – now commonly called learning disability, for example an adult who has the mental age of a child.

3 Substantial impairment of mental responsibility

The effect of the abnormality must be that it *substantially* impairs mental responsibility. Substantial means 'more than trivial, but less than total' according to *R v Lloyd* (1967) and again this is an issue for the jury to decide – whether the abnormality meant the defendant was substantially less responsible for his actions than the ordinary person.

Another defence to murder, reducing the conviction to voluntary manslaughter, is the defence of provocation.

> **Homicide Act 1957 s 3**
>
> 66 *Where on a charge of murder there is evidence on which the jury can find that the person charged was provoked (whether by things done or by things said or both) to lose his self-control, the question whether the provocation was enough to make a reasonable man do as he did shall be left to be determined by the jury; and in determining that question the jury shall take into account everything both done and said according to the effect which, in their opinion, it would have on a reasonable man.* 99

Provocation: Homicide Act 1957 s 3

This defence relies on evidence that:

1. the defendant was provoked
2. this caused a 'sudden, temporary' loss of self-control
3. the jury considers that the reasonable man would also have done as he did.

If there is any evidence capable of amounting to provocation, according to the judge, then it is for the prosecution to prove that the defendant was not provoked in this way, and for the jury to decide the issue.

These elements are explained through case law:

1 The defendant must have been provoked

The provocation may come from things said or done or both. Often the provoking act is something like teasing the defendant, but it can be something as innocent as a baby crying, as shown in *R v Doughty* (1986).

2 This must have caused a sudden, temporary loss of control

The provocation must have caused the defendant to have a 'sudden' loss of control as confirmed in *R v Duffy* (1949). The longer the time-delay or 'cooling off' period between the provocation and the killing, the less likely it is that there was a sudden loss of control. This was shown in *R v Thornton* (1996), where a victim of domestic abuse waited until her husband fell asleep, then sharpened a kitchen knife before returning and stabbing him to death. Also in *R v Ahluwalia* (1992) as described previously. In both cases the defence of diminished responsibility was a more suitable defence, based on the abnormality of mind caused due to battered woman syndrome.

Revenge killings are unlikely to fit the defence as planning makes it less likely that there was a sudden loss of control as in *R v Ibrams and Gregory* (1981).

⊂⊃ links

To find out the full details of the cases mentioned, try using a website such as:

www.a-level-law.com

www.sixthformlaw.info, or

www.bailii.org

Key case

R v Doughty (1986)

The defendant killed his 17-day-old baby whose continual crying made him lose control. His murder conviction was overturned as the judge should have allowed the jury to decide whether the reasonable man would have responded in this way.

3 Reasonable man test

The jury must decide whether the reasonable man would have also been provoked into doing as the defendant did. Often the answer is no, as the 'reasonable' man does not react strongly to minor provocation. If the defendant has a condition that makes him lose control more easily than the reasonable man then the defence of diminished responsibility is more suitable. *In DPP v Camplin* (1978) it was confirmed that the reasonable man would be considered to be of the same age and gender as the defendant. In *R v James and Karimi* (2006) it was confirmed that any characteristics which meant the *effect* of the provocation was more serious on the defendant, than the ordinary person, would be taken into account; but not those characteristics which meant he may lose control more easily than the ordinary person.

Activity

1 Murder/voluntary manslaughter

Are the following guilty of murder or manslaughter? Give your reasons.

a Kimberley was undergoing treatment at a psychiatric hospital as she had begun to hear voices in her head. The voices told her to hit Laken over the head with a baseball bat, which she did, killing her.

b Mitchell was teasing Natalie about a scar on her face, as she got into her car, so she ran him over, killing him.

Involuntary manslaughter

Involuntary manslaughter is where the defendant unlawfully killed someone, but did not have malice aforethought (there was no intent to kill or to cause serious injury). The two main types are: constructive and gross negligence manslaughter.

Constructive/unlawful act manslaughter

To be guilty of this type of involuntary manslaughter, the defendant must have carried out a dangerous criminal act, which caused death.

The three elements of this crime are explained and illustrated in case law as follows:

1 The defendant carried out an unlawful act

The defendant must be committing a crime, which led to the victim's death, but he does not have to realise his actions could result in serious injury or death. He just has to have the *actus reus* and *mens rea* of the original criminal offence – often a battery (intentional or reckless use of unlawful force). This was shown in *R v Mitchell* (1983) where a man pushed another man into an elderly lady, who died as a result of the fall.

2 The unlawful act must be dangerous

The criminal act must be a dangerous act, meaning the ordinary person would realise it carried a risk of *physical* injury. It is irrelevant that the defendant was not aware of the risk of injury, as shown in *DPP v Newbury and Jones* (1976).

3 The unlawful act must have caused the victim's death

As with murder, if it cannot be proved that the defendant's actions caused the death, there is no liability.

R v Ibrams and Gregory (1981)

The defendants had been terrorised by the victim, an ex-boyfriend. They planned to lure him to her, and attack him. They did so and he died. The defence of provocation did not succeed as there was not a 'sudden' loss of control.

DPP v Camplin (1978)

The defendant, Camplin, was a 15-year-old boy who had been sexually abused by the victim, a middle-aged man, who then laughed at him. Camplin hit him over the head with a chapati pan, killing him. Provocation was accepted on appeal, and the court confirmed that he was to be compared to a reasonable boy of his age when deciding if the reasonable person may also have lost control and done as he did.

⦾ links

See page 71 for an example of the principle of transferred malice.

Gross negligence manslaughter

The other main type of involuntary manslaughter is gross negligence manslaughter.

To be guilty of this type of involuntary manslaughter, the defendant must have breached a legal duty of care towards the victim, causing his death, and the breach of duty was 'so bad' in all the circumstances, that a jury considers it should be a criminal offence.

The four elements of this offence are as follows:

1 The defendant owed the victim a legal duty of care

A duty of care may arise in a variety of situations including parents to children; employer to employee; or through contract, as part of a job, as in *R v Pittwood* (1902). It may arise simply because a person ought to have realised that their actions would directly affect the other person.

2 That duty of care was breached

Breach of duty means failing to take reasonable care in the circumstances.

3 The breach of duty must have caused the victim's death

As with other fatal offences, if the defendant's actions did not cause the death, they are not guilty.

4 The jury must consider that the breach of duty constituted 'gross negligence'

If the breach is so serious that it shows a 'disregard for life and safety' and creates an 'obvious, serious risk of death', then the jury may find the defendant guilty. This was shown in *R v Adomako* (1994). Another example is *R v Wacker* (2002), where a lorry driver was smuggling 60 Chinese illegal immigrants in the back of his lorry, without ventilation. He was convicted of manslaughter, as 58 of them died.

Activity

2 Decide if the following are guilty of manslaughter (if so which type), giving your reasons.

a Rana was a registered child-minder. One day he was chatting on the phone and failed to notice that a child he was looking after had wandered out of the garden gate, tried to cross the road and was run over and killed.

b Sarah punched Tara in the face during an argument. Unknown to her, Tara had a genetic condition which made her bruise and cut more easily than other people. The punch caused a gaping wound to her face, which became seriously infected, from which she got blood poisoning and died.

c Victor and his friend Will were young boys of 11 and 12, playing around with his father's airgun, which they thought was not loaded. When Victor pointed the gun at Will, joking, and pulled the trigger, it killed him.

∞ **links**

For a real case based on scenario (c) in the activity box, see the case of *R v Lamb* (1967) at **www.a-level-law.com** under involuntary manslaughter.

■ Evaluation of fatal offences

Murder

1   Some argue that **intent to cause serious injury should not be enough** *mens rea* **for murder.** The **stigma** attached to a murder conviction should not follow a person who did not foresee or intend death. For example, if the defendant intends to break the victim's leg, then he dies from medical complications, this may be murder. On the other hand, it may be argued that the defendant takes this risk when they choose to use serious violence. It would be very difficult for the prosecution to prove they intended death, rather than life-threatening injury.

2   The **mandatory life sentence** is also criticised as it does not take into account the circumstances of the case, which could range from **euthanasia**, to a cold-blooded, sadistic killer.

Voluntary manslaughter

1   The defence of **provocation has been criticised as fitting typical male violence.** As women are usually physically weaker, they rarely lose control and kill 'suddenly', particularly victims of **BWS**, who typically wait for the victim to be in a more vulnerable position. On the other hand, it may be argued that unless a killing is 'sudden' then it is not in response to provocation but is a planned attack and that the law should not allow such defendants to become judge, jury and executioner to the victims.

2   The defence of **diminished responsibility** requires a jury to decide whether a person's mind is 'abnormal', and whether impairment of mental responsibility is 'substantial'. They have little guidance apart from often **conflicting medical evidence**. Also, the defence means some of the most dangerous criminals may receive a lesser sentence, which may not be the best way to protect society.

Involuntary manslaughter

1   **Constructive manslaughter** allows a person who did **not realise the risk of any injury at all** to be guilty of manslaughter. If the reasonable person foresaw a risk of some physical injury, this is enough for a conviction.

2   **Gross negligence manslaughter** allows a person who **did not have any criminal** *mens rea* **at all** to be guilty of manslaughter. A defendant has no way of knowing whether what they did was a crime, until their case is decided in court by that individual jury.

Key terms

Stigma: bad reputation because of society's disapproval.

Euthanasia: where the defendant killed the victim at their own request, to avoid intense suffering due to a terminal illness.

BWS: battered woman syndrome, affecting victims of long-term domestic abuse.

AQA Examiner's tip

■ When answering a fatal offence question, tell the examiner what words in the question lead you to believe the defendant had the necessary elements of the offence you think they committed.

■ The key to distinguishing between murder and involuntary manslaughter is lack of intent to kill or seriously injure.

Learning summary

You should now be able to:

demonstrate an understanding of murder

demonstrate an understanding of voluntary manslaughter

demonstrate an understanding of involuntary manslaughter.

7.3 Non-fatal offences against the person

These are the main offences against the person: common assault (assault or battery); assault occasioning actual bodily harm (ABH); unlawful, malicious wounding or infliction of grievous bodily harm (GBH) without, or with intent.

▌Common assault

This is a **common law offence** which may consist of assault or battery or both. Common assault is charged under the Criminal Justice Act 1988 s 39 and carries a six-month maximum sentence.

Assault

Although the word 'assault' may be used in the everyday sense, to cover all offences of violence, it actually has a technical legal meaning.

> The legal meaning of assault is:
>
> To intentionally or recklessly cause a person to apprehend (anticipate or fear) immediate, unlawful force.

Therefore, to commit the offence of assault, there need be no touching involved at all, as it is any action or words which cause a person to think you are *about to* attack them. Menacing silence may be enough for assault, as in *R v Ireland* (1997), although it is usually caused by threatening words or an action such as raising a fist or pulling a weapon.

There is no assault if the words themselves assure the victim that they will *not* be attacked. This was the case in *Turberville v Savage* (1669), where the defendant made it clear that if the judge had not been in town, he would have stabbed the victim with his sword.

Battery

The word 'battery' sounds far worse than it actually is. It need be no more than an unauthorised touch, although the court will assume we consent to a certain amount of contact in everyday activities.

> The legal definition of battery is: to intentionally or recklessly use unlawful force on a person.

Collins v Wilcock (1984) shows that grabbing a person's arm may be battery. If the force (or contact) used causes no injury or only **trivial** injury, then this is battery. Battery can be committed without directly touching a person also, for example, spitting or throwing a stone or setting a trap.

Assault occasioning actual bodily harm (ABH)

This offence is charged under the Offences Against the Person Act 1861 s 47, carrying a maximum sentence of five years' imprisonment.

Objectives

In this topic you will learn:

how to demonstrate an understanding of the definition and key elements of common assault (assault and battery)

how to demonstrate an understanding of the definition and key elements of assault occasioning actual bodily harm

how to demonstrate an understanding of the definition and key elements of grievous bodily harm and wounding (with and without intent).

⊂⊃ links

See Topic 6.3 to understand how the crimes of assault and battery are defined in the same way, and using many of the same cases, in the tort of trespass to the person.

Key case — *R v Ireland* (1997)

The defendant made a series of menacing silent phone calls, which caused the victim to fear he may attack her at any time. This was an assault although he had not even touched her. He intentionally caused her to apprehend force.

Key case — *Collins v Wilcock* (1984)

A police officer grabbed a woman's arm to attract her attention. This was unlawful force, so she was entitled to defend herself, as the officer could have used other methods to attract attention.

ABH has been defined as an assault or a battery that caused 'any injury calculated to interfere with the health or comfort' of the victim (*R v Miller* (1954))

or

an assault or battery that has caused 'harm which is not so trivial as to be wholly insignificant' (*R v Chan Fook* (1994)).

The word 'assault' here means either an assault or a battery. The word 'occasioning' means 'causing'. The phrase 'actual bodily harm' is defined above. The only *mens rea* that must be proved is that the defendant intentionally or recklessly carried out an assault or battery, so there is no need to intend or foresee any *injury*, as confirmed in *R v Savage* (1991).

Unlawful, malicious wounding or infliction of grievous bodily harm (wounding/GBH without intent)

This offence is charged under the Offences Against the Person Act 1861 s 20, and carries a maximum sentence of five years' imprisonment.

Section 20 wounding/GBH without intent is:

to inflict a wound or grievous bodily harm, intending or being reckless that *some* harm may occur.

The *actus reus* can, therefore, be causing *either* a wound *or* grievous bodily harm but not necessarily both.

A wound is defined as a 'break in the continuity of the whole skin' in *JCC v Eisenhower* (1984). Minor scratches are unlikely to be classed as wounds, but more serious cuts may be.

Grievous bodily harm is defined as 'serious injury' in *R v Saunders* (1985). This can either be physical (such as broken bones) or psychiatric injury.

The *mens rea* 'maliciously' means to intend or be reckless that *some* harm may be caused, as confirmed in *R v Mowatt* (1967). There is no need to intend or foresee **serious harm**.

Key cases

R v Savage (1991)

A woman threw beer at her ex-boyfriend's new girlfriend, and the beer glass flew out of her hand and caused minor injury to the victim's arm. Throwing beer is a battery as it is intentional use of unlawful force, and the battery caused actual bodily harm. It did not matter that she did not intend or foresee any injury might occur.

R v Roberts (1971)

A woman suffered injuries when she jumped from a moving car, due to the defendant's unwanted sexual advances. He was found guilty of causing ABH.

links

See Topic 7.1 for a recap on the meaning of *actus reus* and *mens rea*.

Key cases

JCC v Eisenhower (1984)

There was no wounding when the defendant shot the victim in the eye with an airgun as there was no break in the skin, only broken blood vessels or internal bleeding.

R v Burstow (1997)

A sustained campaign of harassment, including stalking, caused a woman to suffer severe depressive illness. This was sufficient to amount to GBH as it was serious harm.

Unlawful, malicious wounding or causing of grievous bodily harm (wounding/GBH with intent)

This offence is charged under the Offences Against the Person Act 1861 s 18, and carries a maximum sentence of life imprisonment. The offence has exactly the same *actus reus* as in s 20, and is committed when the defendant causes a wound or GBH, but the *mens rea* is different. It must be shown that the defendant either **intended** *serious* **injury** or intended to prevent/resist lawful arrest. If a person causes serious injury by intentionally using severe force or a weapon, for example, it is likely that they may be guilty of s 18 GBH with intent.

A *Non-fatal offences against the person*

Offence	Section and Act	Actus reus	Mens rea	Case examples
Assault	Criminal Justice Act 1988 s 39	To cause apprehension of immediate, unlawful force	Intention or recklessness that the victim would be caused this apprehension of force	*R* v *Ireland* (1997) (silent phone calls)
Battery	Criminal Justice Act 1988 s 39	To use unlawful force on a person	Intention or recklessness that unlawful force would be used	*Collins* v *Wilcock* (1984) (grabbed shoulder)
Assault occasioning actual bodily harm	Offences Against the Person Act 1861 s 47	To carry out an assault or battery which has caused actual bodily harm (more than trivial injury)	Intention or recklessness that an assault or battery would occur (no need to intend or foresee any injury)	*R* v *Savage* (1991) (threw beer and glass injured victim)
Unlawful, malicious wounding or infliction of grievous bodily harm without intent	Offences Against the Person Act 1861 s 20	To cause a wound (break in the skin) or to cause GBH (serious injury)	Intention or recklessness to cause some harm (no need to intend or foresee serious harm)	*JCC* v *Eisenhower* (1984) (broken blood vessels not a wound) *R* v *Burstow* (1987) (serious psychiatric harm caused by harrassment)
Unlawful, malicious wounding or causing of grievous bodily harm with intent	Offences Against the Person Act 1861 s 18	To cause a wound (break in the skin) or to cause GBH (serious injury)	Intention to cause serious injury or to prevent/resist lawful arrest	*R* v *Belfon* (1976) (severe injuries due to slashing with razor)

Activity

1 Non-fatal offences against the person

Which offences, if any, have been committed in the following situations? Give reasons for your decision.

a Rachel whispered in Ben's ear that if he wasn't wearing glasses, she would punch him.

b Adam pulled a knife on Carl and threatened to stab him.

c Akmal silently crept up behind Jamal and shouted 'boo!', making him jump.

d Paul slipped on a banana skin and fell into Clifford, knocking him over but causing no injury.

e Dan threatened to beat Ellie up and chased her. She ran across the road to escape and was hit by a bike, suffering concussion.

f Fifi deliberately stabbed Georgina in the chest with a knife, causing deep cuts which needed surgery.

g Harry kicked Imogen in the leg, causing a red mark.

h Kelly slapped Liam's face and a ring she was wearing caused a deep gash in his cheek.

i Mo hit Neil on the head with a hammer, causing brain injury.

j Omar spat at Penny.

Evaluating non-fatal offences

▪ The law relating to non-fatal offences is mostly contained in an Act of Parliament which is centuries old. Many of the **words used in the names and definitions of these offences are no longer in use** and so are confusing, e.g. '**bodily**', '**occasioning**', and '**grievous**'. Judges have had to interpret the words used, to give them up-to-date meanings and to fit new situations. Many argue it is now time for Parliament to pass an updated Act so that current definitions are made clear.

▪ A further criticism of the current law is that the **structure of the maximum sentences does not reflect the blameworthiness** of the defendants. For example, the offences of assault occasioning actual bodily harm and unlawful, malicious infliction of grievous bodily harm without intent carry the same 5-year maximum sentence. Also, the maximum life sentence for causing grievous bodily harm with intent is the same as for murder.

▪ The legal or technical definitions of these offences means a person may be guilty of a crime by simply shouting 'boo!' (assault) or by simply stroking a person's cheek (battery), or by a minor cut to someone's finger (wounding). However, in reality, the police are unlikely to charge these offences for such simple actions. The **theory does not match the practice**, as shown in the joint charging standard.

The joint charging standard

Not every action which technically, in law, constitutes an offence, will *actually* be charged as one in practice. It may be a waste of police time to charge a person with assault for shouting 'boo!' So, although in your exams *you* will be required to consider every possible offence that could technically have been committed, in real life, the police may make a different decision.

To assist police in deciding which offence to charge for specific types of injury, a joint standard was agreed with the Crown Prosecution Service.

Examples of injuries which may be charged as common assault include: grazes, scratches, minor bruising, swelling, reddening of skin, superficial cuts, black eye.

Examples of injuries which may be charged as ABH include: loss of teeth; temporary unconsciousness; extensive bruising; broken nose; minor fractures; minor cuts requiring stitches; psychiatric injury which is more than ordinary fear or distress.

Examples of injuries which may be charged as GBH include: permanent loss of sensory function (e.g. reduced ability to see, hear, touch, smell etc.); permanent disfigurement (e.g. scarring); broken bones; fractured skull; wounds requiring blood transfusion or injuries requiring lengthy treatment.

Key terms

Bodily: in ABH/GBH this means harm to either body or mind.

Occasioning: in ABH this means 'causing'.

Grievous: in GBH this means 'serious'.

Law Commission: a body set up to advise the government on changes that need to be made to the law.

AQA   Examiner's tip

If you use definitions and cases to back up your answers this will have a positive effect on your marks. For example, rather than just saying 'When Harry kicked Sally this was battery,' you should then continue to say: 'because he intentionally used unlawful force, as shown in *Collins* v *Wilcock* (1984), where grabbing someone's shoulder was battery.'

Did you know ???????

Under Crime and Disorder Act 1998 s 29 , if any of the non-fatal offences are racially aggravated (meaning the reason for the attack was a person's race), then the sentence may be increased by up to two years.

Learning summary

You should now be able to:

demonstrate an understanding of common assault (assault and battery)

demonstrate an understanding of assault occasioning actual bodily harm (ABH)

demonstrate an understanding of grievous bodily harm (GBH) and wounding, with or without intent.

Offences against property

Probably the most well-known property offence is theft. Most people know what theft is, but do you know the difference between theft and robbery? Or between robbery and burglary?

> Theft is defined in Theft Act 1968 s 1 as:
>
> 'dishonestly appropriat[ing] property belonging to another with the intention of permanently depriving the other of it'.

■ Theft

Taking each part in turn, this means:

1 Dishonestly

According to the case of *R* v *Ghosh* (1982), the magistrates or jury will decide if they believe the defendant realised s/he was acting dishonestly according to the standards of ordinary people.

Although the Theft Act 1968 does not define honesty, it does give examples of situation which are *not* dishonest:

1 if you believed you had a legal right to the property, e.g. if you thought it was yours
2 if you believed you would have had the owner's consent
3 if you took reasonable steps to find the owner and believed they could not be found.

2 Appropriate

To appropriate something means to act as if you were the owner of the property – 'to assume the rights of ownership'.

Very often a theft involves *taking* something that doesn't belong to you, but there are many ways of appropriating property which may not involve physically picking the property up at all.

3 Property

Certain things will not be considered 'property' in theft law, although they may be covered by other offences. These include electricity, wild foliage or animals (unless appropriated for commercial purposes), land, and even corpses!

4 Intent to permanently deprive

It must be shown that the defendant did not intend to return the property. Borrowing will not amount to theft, unless it can be shown that there was a dishonest intention never to return it. There are some exceptions to this rule, such as if the whole of the value of the item has been used, e.g. if a season ticket is stolen and used, then the ticket is returned or if a person takes property then sells it back to its owner, this is still theft.

Objectives

In this topic you will learn:

how to demonstrate an understanding of theft

how to demonstrate an understanding of robbery

how to demonstrate an understanding of burglary

how to demonstrate an understanding of making off without payment.

Key case

***R v Morris* (1984)**

The defendant switched price tickets, intending to pay a lower amount. This was an appropriation even if he did not get to the checkout, as it is the owner's right to price their own goods.

Activity

1 Appropriation

Make a list of all the things an owner of property has the right to do with that property.

Remember

Assuming rights over someone else's property is 'appropriating' it. Don't forget, however, that this must be done 'dishonestly' to be theft.

Key case

***Oxford v Moss* (1979)**

Students read exam papers before the exam took place, then put them back. As information is not 'property' this was not theft. (Beware – there are other offences that may be committed, just not the crime of theft!)

The crime of 'taking a vehicle without consent' (TWOC)

When a person takes a vehicle without consent they do not have the intent to permanently deprive, as they are 'joyriding' and intend to abandon the vehicle. This would not be theft of the car, but a separate crime known as TWOC.

■ Robbery

> The definition of robbery is found in Theft Act 1968 s 8:
>
> Robbery is to steal, 'and immediately before or at the time of doing so, and in order to do so, [using] force on any person or [putting or seeking to put] any person in fear of being then and there subjected to force.'

Taking each aspect in turn:

1 To steal

If there is no theft, there is no robbery either!

2 To use force or fear of force in order to steal

This is what turns theft into robbery – the element of force or fear. In *R v Dawson* (1976) the defendant nudged the victim hard enough for him to lose his balance, so he could take his wallet, and this was enough force to be robbery.

3 The timing of the force/threat of force must be immediately before or during the theft

The force or threat of force must be used in order for the theft to take place. Therefore, the force must be used just before or during the theft. If there is theft and violence is used separately, then this is not robbery, but theft, and an offence against the person. However, if the act of theft is still continuing when the force is used, then this will be robbery, as in *R v Hale* (1978), where one burglar was upstairs committing theft and the other was downstairs tying the victim up.

Key case

R v Lloyd (1985)

The defendant took cinema films home to illegally copy them, then returned them before he was caught out. This act is illegal but is not theft, as the films had already been returned so there was no intent to permanently deprive.

AQA Examiner's tip

A person can have the intent to permanently deprive, even if they are prevented from carrying it out, e.g. if they are caught on the spot.

∞ links

See Topic 7.1 for information *actus reus* and *mens rea*. Make sure you can pick out from these definitions what the *actus reus* and *mens rea* of theft and robbery are.

Activities

2 Theft – are the following examples of theft or not? Give reasons for your decisions.

a Amy uses her flatmate Russell's milk, without asking.

b Carly finds a £10 note in the street and decides to keep it.

c Margaret advertises Flo's car for sale, without her permission, then takes the money for it.

d Holly goes joyriding in Ian's car without him knowing, then leaves it in a field and walks home.

3 Consider whether the following may be guilty of robbery, giving your reasons:

a Sheniz punched Asif in the face, and while he was on the floor, Charlotte grabbed his wallet and ran off with it.

b Chennelle threatened bank staff with her dad's air rifle, and demanded cash, but staff pushed the panic button and she was arrested before she could take anything.

c Jake grabbed Mike's mobile phone from the desk and ran off, then ran back and punched Mike in the face.

Burglary

What is the difference between robbery and burglary? Often people use both words in the same way and say they were robbed when they were really burgled.

The definition of burglary is found in Theft Act 1968 s 9.

> Section 9(1)(a) To enter a building or part, as a trespasser, with intent to commit theft, GBH or unlawful damage, OR
>
> Section 9(1)(b) To enter as a trespasser and then committing/attempt theft or GBH.

The elements of burglary are therefore:

1 To enter a building or part of a building

It cannot be burglary unless the defendant has made substantial entry to a building or part of a building. The courts have been quite generous in their interpretation of a building, however, as shown in *B and S v Leathley* (1979), where an old outdoor freezer was considered to be a 'building'.

It may be just a *part* of a building where the defendant is not authorised to be.

2 As a trespasser

A trespasser is a person who does not have permission to be on the owner's land.

3 Either with intent to commit theft, GBH or damage once inside

Most people know that burglary usually involves intention to steal – but not many people know that there may be no theft involved at all. Entering the building intending to cause serious injury to someone or to commit unlawful damage are alternative forms of *mens rea*.

If you have one of these three things in mind as you enter the building, you have committed section 9(1)(a) burglary. This may be difficult to prove if you have not actually attempted to do any of those things, since it relies on what the jury believes you intended as you entered.

4 Or entering without intent but actually stealing or committing GBH once inside

Section 9(1)(b) burglary is easier to prove as there is no need to prove any mens rea on entry to the building, but it must be shown that once inside, there was at least an attempt to steal or to cause GBH.

Did you know ??????

If you trespassed with intent to rape this used to be burglary, but this has now been changed by the Sexual Offences Act 2003. Older textbooks may still have reference to intent to rape as part of burglary.

Activity

4 **Burglary**

Which is easier to prove, and why: section 9(1)(a) burglary or section 9(1)(b) burglary?

Key case

R v Walkington (1979)

The defendant went behind the counter in a shop, to look through drawers to see if there was anything to steal. He was a trespasser at that point as he was in a part of the building he had no permission to be in. As he had the intent to steal, this was burglary.

links

See Topic 7.1 for a recap on the meanings of *actus reus* and *mens rea*. Section 9(1)(a) and (b) require *mens rea* to be formed at different times – the first is on entry to the building and the other is once inside the building.

A *Costumed burglars are easier to spot*

Making off without payment

Under Theft Act 1978 s 3 a person is guilty of this offence if:

knowing that payment on the spot for goods or services is required or expected of him, he dishonestly makes off without paying and with intent to avoid payment.

Examples of making off without payment include:

- at petrol stations, where the driver leaves with the intention of avoiding payment for the petrol put into his car
- at restaurants, where the diner leaves with the intention of avoiding payment for the meal
- in hotels, where the guest leaves with the intention of avoiding payment of the bill.

In *R v Brooks and Brooks* (1983), the defendants took a taxi ride for 13 miles to their home then refused to pay, so the driver drove them to a police station, where they ran away. They argued that as payment was required 'on the spot,' at the end of the destination (their home), they had not 'made off' from that spot, but from the police station. Inventive logic, but the court found them guilty anyway, as you would expect!

Activity

6 Offences against property

Make a table like this one, filling in the blanks:

Offence	Actus reus	Mens rea	Case example
Theft		To act dishonestly and with intent to permanently deprive	*R v Morris* (1984) – switching price labels to pay a lower price is theft
T.W.O.C.	To take a vehicle (not including a pushbike) belonging to another		Not required
Robbery	To steal and use force or fear of force in order to steal	To act dishonestly and with intent to permanently deprive	
Burglary		S 9(1)(a) intent, on entry, to steal; GBH; damage S 9(1)(b) having entered, intent to steal or GBH	*R v Walkington* (1979) – being in an unauthorised part of a building is enough for *actus reus* of burglary
Making off without payment	To 'make off' or leave a place where payment on the spot is required, without paying		

Activity

5 Burglary

Decide whether the following may be guilty of burglary and if so, which type, giving your reasons:

a Kerrie and Jeff decided to go and have a look round an old, unused building. When they got in, through a broken window, they saw an antique table and chairs set and decided to take it and do it up, to sell.

b Russell and Chris planned to steal a rare Persian cat by sneaking in through their neighbour's unlocked door, while they were at work. The cat was nowhere to be seen so they left empty-handed.

c Abbi sneaked onto her boyfriend's houseboat while he was asleep, intending to break his legs with a baseball bat, as he was cheating on her. He woke up and took the bat from her before she could do anything.

d Bill put his arm through a letterbox and reached over to the hooks by the door, taking Tracey's car keys.

e Dave and Les went into the wrong house through an unlocked door, while they were drunk, thinking it was their own. Once inside they made some toast and fell asleep.

Learning summary

You should now be able to:

demonstrate an understanding of theft

demonstrate an understanding of robbery

demonstrate an understanding of burglary

demonstrate an understanding of making off without payment.

Insanity

The defence of insanity is explained in *M'Naghten's case* (1843). Three things must be proved:

1 The defendant must have been suffering from a 'disease of the mind'

A *Disease of the mind – a legal rather than a medical term*

Examples of 'disease of the mind'	Meaning	Case example	Details
Diabetes	If in hyperglycaemic state (naturally occurring high blood sugar in diabetics) this can affect the mind	*R v Hennessey* (1989)	The defendant stole a car whilst in a hyperglycaemic state
Arteriosclerosis	Hardening arteries – if these are to the brain, the mind can be affected	*R v Kemp* (1957)	The defendant attacked his wife with a hammer while suffering from hardening arteries to the brain
Epilepsy	During a seizure an epileptic may not be in control of their actions	*R v Sullivan* (1984)	The defendant punched and kicked the victim during the initial stages of a seizure
Somnambulism	The correct name for sleepwalking	*R v Burgess* (1991)	The defendant attacked his girlfriend with a bottle and video recorder and tried to strangle her, in his sleep
Conditions which will NOT be classed as diseases of the mind	External factors such as alcohol or drugs; a blow to the head or hypnotism alter the functioning of the mind, but will not be classed as insanity – more likely to be intoxication or automatism	*R v Quick* (1973)	A diabetic nurse attacked a patient while in a hypoglycaemic state (low blood sugar due to taking insulin but not eating properly afterwards). The court said this is an external cause and so not insanity but may be automatism

2 This disease must have caused a 'defect of reason'

Defects of reason must be more than merely absent-mindedness as shown in *R v Clarke* (1972), where an elderly lady forgot to pay for her shopping. Powers of rational decision-making must be so seriously affected that it causes one of the results below.

3 *Either* they did not know the 'nature and quality' of their act, *or* they did not know it was wrong

They must either not know what they are doing or not know it is legally wrong. If successful, the result is the 'special verdict' of 'not guilty by reason of insanity'. If the crime charged was murder, then the defendant will be ordered to a secure hospital but for other crimes; this is at the judge's discretion.

Automatism

To successfully plead this defence, the defendant must be shown to have committed an 'act done by the muscles of the body without control of the mind' (*Bratty v A-G* (1963)). Actions must be totally, not merely partially, involuntary, as confirmed in *Hill v Baxter* (1958) and must be due to an external cause, e.g. hypnosis.

Objectives

In this topic you will learn:

how to demonstrate an outline understanding of insanity, automatism, intoxication, duress, circumstances/necessity, self-defence and consent.

Key terms

Specific intent: crimes where a specific intent (not recklessness) is required, e.g. murder intent to kill.

Basic intent: crimes where the *mens rea* includes recklessness.

Key case

R v Sullivan (1984)

The defendant had an epileptic seizure, during which he caused the victim serious injury. He was found not guilty by reason of insanity as epilepsy may be considered a 'disease of the mind'.

Intoxication

B *Intoxication through alcohol or drugs*

Type of intoxication	Meaning	Effect	Case examples
Voluntary intoxication	The defendant willingly took substances known to cause intoxication	Will be a defence only to crimes of **specific intent**, if that intent was not formed because of the intoxication. If accepted, guilty of lesser offence e.g. s 18 GBH reduced to s 20 GBH	*DPP* v *Majewski* (1976) The intoxicated defendant attacked a number of victims. Defence rejected as these assaults were crimes of basic intent (could be committed recklessly and he already showed recklessness by being intoxicated)
Involuntary intoxication	The defendant was unaware that he had taken substances which cause intoxication, e.g. spiked drinks or side-effects of prescription drugs	May be a defence to crimes of specific and **basic intent** if *mens rea* is not formed. If accepted, verdict is not guilty	*R* v *Hardie* (1985) The defendant set fire to his friend's flat after taking his friend's prescription drug Valium, not knowing it can cause aggression in some people. Defence accepted

Duress (by threats)

Duress is a defence where a person is forced to commit a crime because of threats of serious injury or death. The defence is not available to a charge of murder or attempted murder, as a matter of principle. This was shown in *R* v *Gotts* (1992) where the defence was rejected when the defendant attempted to kill his mother due to threats by his father that he would kill him if he did not.

Duress of circumstances/necessity

This is a defence where a person is forced, due to the *circumstances*, to commit a crime, to prevent some greater harm. Like duress by threats, it is not available to a murder charge. If it is accepted, the result is not guilty. The defence was accepted in *R* v *Conway* (1989) where the defendant committed driving offences while trying to escape what he feared were potential attackers.

Self-defence

This defence is accepted where the defendant used 'reasonable' force in order to defend himself or someone over whom he had responsibility or his property. The amount of force used must be proportionate to the threat of force from the victim.

Consent

This defence is accepted on the basis that the victim gave permission for the act to be carried out. It is only accepted, however, if there is no injury caused, unless the activity falls within a 'lawful exception' category, for example: ear-piercing, tattooing, surgery, dangerous sports or rough games. This defence was accepted in *R* v *Aiken* (1992) where RAF officers caused serious burns by setting fire to one another's fireproof suits.

Key case

Hill v *Baxter* (1958)

The defendant claimed to have committed driving offences due to automatism as he was 'driving without awareness'. However, the court rejected this defence, as his actions were not totally involuntary as he was still driving the car. The judge gave examples of what would have been considered automatism, including the theoretical example of a swarm of bees flying in the car, which would cause the driver to act involuntarily.

Learning summary

You should now be able to:

demonstrate an outline understanding of the general defences to crime: insanity, automatism, intoxication, duress by threats or circumstances/necessity, self-defence and consent.

7

You should now be able to:

✔ demonstrate an understanding of the principles of criminal liability

✔ demonstrate an understanding of the definition and key elements of fatal offences, non-fatal offences and property offences

✔ demonstrate an understanding of the general defences to crime.

Revision questions

1. What is the literal translation and the actual meaning of the term *actus reus*?

2. What is the literal translation and the actual meaning of the term *mens rea*?

3. What does intent mean?

4. What does recklessness mean?

5. When can a person be criminally liable for an omission (failure to act)?

6. What does the thin skull rule mean?

7. What does transferred malice mean?

8. What is the *actus reus* of assault?

9. What is the *actus reus* of battery?

10. Why was the defendant in *Collins* v *Wilcock* (1984) allowed to defend herself when she was grabbed?

11. What did the defendant do in *R* v *Ireland* (1998) which was assault?

12. What is the *mens rea* for assault occasioning actual bodily harm?

13. Did the defendant in *R* v *Savage* (1991) commit an assault or a battery which led to actual bodily harm?

14. What is the difference between a s 18 and a s 20 offence of wounding/GBH?

15. What does GBH stand for?

16. What is the definition of a wound?

17. Why was the defendant not guilty of wounding in *JCC* v *Eisenhower* (1987)?

18. What is the definition of murder?

19. What is malice aforethought?

20. Name the three defences to murder under the Homicide Act 1957.

21. Name the three things that must be proved to have the defence of provocation accepted.

22. Name the three things that must be proved to have the defence of diminished responsibility accepted.

23. What is voluntary manslaughter?

24. What is involuntary manslaughter?

25. Name the two types of involuntary manslaughter.

26. Name the three things that must be proved for a person to be guilty of constructive manslaughter.

27. Name the four things that must be proved for a person to be guilty of gross negligence manslaughter.

28. Name the three things that must be proved for a person to have the defence of insanity accepted.

29. What happened in the *M'Naghten* case?

30. What is the difference between the results of a successful defence of insanity and the defence of automatism?

31. What are the two types of intoxication and which is more likely to succeed as a defence?

32. What is an offence of specific intent?

33. What is an offence of basic intent?

34. Why was the defence of intoxication rejected in *DPP* v *Majewski* (1976)?

35. How much force can be used in self-defence?

36. What example of automatism was given in *Hill* v *Baxter* (1958)?

37. Why was the defendant in *R* v *Hardie* (1985) not guilty of criminal damage?

38. Which is easier to prove and why: s 9(1)(a) burglary or s 9(1)(b)?

What you should already know:

✔ the structure of courts operating in England and Wales (Chapter 1).

Chapter contents

Introduction to family law

In this chapter, we shall be examining the important elements of family law. You might be surprised to know that the law plays an important part in marriage, with a number of rules which must be obeyed.

More obviously, you are likely to be aware that the law plays an important role when a marriage comes to an end, both in terms of the divorce and also in terms of dealing with the financial consequences of that divorce. You may remember the recent divorce settlement involving Paul and Heather Mills-McCartney which reputedly ran into millions of pounds.

The law also plays an important role when someone dies, in that their possessions (estate) needs to be dealt with, whether the deceased has made a will or not.

Definition of marriage

'The voluntary union for life by one man and one woman to the exclusion of all others': *Hyde* v *Hyde* (1866).

In this country marriage is **monogamous**, i.e. one man and one woman. Certain countries, e.g. Saudi Arabia, and certain religions, e.g. Islam, allow **polygamy**, i.e. multiple wives. Some religions also permit **polyandry**, i.e. multiple husbands.

The requirements of a valid marriage

Both parties must be at least 16 years of age

If either party is under 18, **consent** must be given by the minors' parents, if alive. If permission is refused, the minor may apply to the Magistrates' Court, where magistrates make a decision based on the best interests of the minor, e.g. where a minor girl is pregnant, permission may be granted.

Prohibited degrees

Marriage is not allowed between parties within the **prohibited degrees**. This means that certain persons who are closely related, either by blood or marriage, may not marry each other, e.g. parents/ children, brother/sister, etc.

The Marriage Act 1949, as amended by the Marriage (Enabling) Act 1960, provides two complete lists of the prohibited degrees. The reason for these prohibitions is, first, public policy, and secondly, the risk of genetic disabilities in any children.

Neither party must have an existing marriage

A person who marries for a second time whilst the first marriage is in existence may commit the crime of **bigamy** (Offences Against the Person Act 1857 s 57), although the following defences may be pleaded:

- that in good faith and on reasonable grounds it was believed that the spouse was dead, or that the first marriage was annulled or dissolved
- that the first spouse had been missing continuously for seven years and there was no reason for supposing that the first spouse was alive.

Both parties must be of sound mind

This is governed by the Mental Health Act 1983.

The legal formalities required by statute

There are two different legal ways of getting married under English law, both governed by the Marriage Act 1949 as amended.

Objectives

In this topic you will learn:

how to describe the legal requirements of a valid marriage

how to describe the law relating to void and voidable marriages

how to outline the law relating to civil partnerships

how to discuss critically the law on marriage and civil partnerships.

∞ links

Government website on family law/divorce: **www.gro.gov.uk/gro/ content/marriages**

Key terms

Prohibited degrees: close relations who cannot marry.

Bigamy: marrying someone whilst already married.

Banns: announcements in church of a forthcoming marriage.

Key case

R v Tolson (1889)

A husband deserted his wife in 1881. The wife heard from reliable sources that the husband had been drowned. The wife remarried in 1887. Later that year, the husband reappeared. The wife was charged with bigamy.

The court decided that, even though the wife (Mrs Tolson) had not waited seven years as she should have done, she honestly believed that the husband, Mr Tolson, was dead. Therefore, she was acquitted.

You might think this is a fair and sensible decision.

The Church of England

The procedure to be followed by a couple wishing to have a Church of England wedding must be chosen from one of the following four:

1. Marriage by banns

This is the traditional method. The **banns** are an announcement of the intended marriage, read out on three successive Sundays in the parish churches of both parties. A person may then object to the marriage for a valid reason, e.g. parents of a minor.

2. Marriage by common licence

This is on the authority of the local Bishop. There is a 15-day residence requirement.

3. Marriage by special licence

Only the Archbishop of Canterbury can grant special licences, in urgent cases. The parties may marry anywhere and at any time, e.g. in hospital, when one of the parties is dying.

4. Marriage by Superintendent Registrar's certificate

This is very rarely used for Church of England weddings.

A *A typical church wedding*

■ Civil ceremony

All other marriages, including civil marriages in a register office, Roman Catholic or Jewish marriages, etc., are authorised by the **Superintendent Registrar**.

Marriage by Superintendent Registrar's certificate

The Superintendent Registrar is commonly the Registrar of Births, Marriages and Deaths.

Notice of the intended marriage must be given to the Registrar in the districts in which the parties have lived for seven days before giving notice. The notice is then published. If after 15 days no objection has been made, the certificate is issued.

The marriage must take place in the register office or in 'a building registered for the purpose'. Such buildings include a Roman Catholic church, synagogue, temple etc. Under the Marriage Act 1994, civil ceremonies may now take place on approved premises, usually premises licensed by the local authority. Applications for such licences have been received from places as diverse as stately homes, football clubs and Blackpool Tower.

Only authorised persons may conduct the marriage: usually the minister or other official from the particular religion, or the Superintendent Registrar. As with Church of England weddings, **two witnesses** must be present, the marriage must take place between **8.00 am and 6.00 pm**, and the ceremony must be **open to the public**.

Registrar General's licence

If someone is suffering from a fatal illness and is anxious to marry, but cannot be moved to a church or register office, the Registrar-General can grant a licence to permit the marriage, e.g. in hospital.

Civil partnerships

The Civil Partnership Act 2004 was implemented on 5 December 2005. This enables same-sex couples to obtain legal recognition of their relationship as 'civil partners'. Civil partners will have equal treatment with married couples in a wide range of legal matters, including:

- tax, including inheritance tax
- employment benefits
- duty to provide reasonable maintenance for one's civil partner and any children
- ability to apply for parental responsibility for one's civil partner's child
- recognition under intestacy rules
- protection from domestic violence.

A civil partnership requires notice, similar to the notice rules relating to marriage. A civil partnership can be formed in England and Wales at a register office or approved premises.

<aside>
Key terms

Void marriage: a marriage that has never existed.

Voidable marriage: a marriage that can be annulled (ended) by a court order – not to be confused with the dissolution (ending) of a marriage by divorce (see Topic 8.2).
</aside>

B *A same-sex civil partnership, legal since 2005*

Nullity of marriage

A marriage that appears to be entirely valid may, in fact, be either **void** or **voidable**. A void marriage is one that despite appearances is never legally a marriage. A voidable marriage is one that begins as a valid marriage but is liable to be annulled by a court. The Court involved is the High Court (Family Division). Both void and voidable marriages are governed by the Matrimonial Causes Act 1973.

Void marriages

A marriage will be void if any of the following circumstances applies to it:

- if either party is under 16 years of age: if either party is aged 16 and 17 and permission has not been granted then the marriage is valid but the parties may be prosecuted for fraud

<aside>
AQA *Examiner's tip*

Make sure you fully understand the difference between a void and a voidable marriage.

When 16/17 year-olds marry without consent, many think the marriage is void. In fact the marriage is **valid,** but a fraud prosecution could follow.
</aside>

- if either party is already married
- if the parties are closely related
- if the parties are not respectively male and female: sex change operations do not alter one's legal gender
- if both parties knew when marrying of some legal irregularity, e.g. if wedding was not solemnised by an authorised person, banns were not published, etc.

Voidable marriages

A court may annul an existing marriage by making a decree of nullity in the following cases:

- if a party is unable or unwilling to consummate the marriage
- if at the time of the marriage either party was suffering from mental disorder (Mental Health Act 1983)
- if the wife at the time of the marriage was pregnant by another man and the husband did not know
- if a party was at the time of the marriage suffering from a communicable venereal disease
- if either party had not genuinely consented, e.g. a 'shotgun wedding', or if one of the parties was too drunk to consent.

Nullity proceedings must be instituted within three years of the date of the marriage.

C 'Drunk! Who says I'm drunk?'

> **Remember**
>
> That you should support your answers in examinations with legal authority. In this area, this means learning and citing the different Acts of Parliament. In particular, you should refer to the Marriage Acts 1949 and 1994, the Matrimonial Causes Act 1973 and the Civil Partnership Act 2004.

Activity

1 Criticisms of the law relating to marriage

You may care to consider the following points. A class debate may be a good way of sorting out the issue and helping you to remember it. Remember, there are no right or wrong answers, but a good discussion always looks at both points of view.

a Are the legal requirements of a marriage still good law today? For example, the age limits, bigamous marriages, time limits (8.00 am to 6.00 pm), etc.

b Why are there restrictions on the place of marriage? Surely an authorised person to conduct the wedding should be enough?

c Should civil partners have the same rights as married couples?

d Are the categories of void and voidable marriages appropriate?

> **Did you know** ??????
>
> In 1972, there were 480,285 marriages in the UK. That number had fallen to 275,140 by 2006. Why do you think there has been such a large fall?

> **AQA Examiner's tip**
>
> You do not need to write a lot to successfully answer family law questions in an examination – but you do need to be *accurate*.

Learning summary

You should now be able to:

describe accurately the requirements of a valid marriage and legal implications of a civil partnership

describe both void and voidable marriages.

8.2 Divorce

The law on divorce

The party applying for the divorce is called the **petitioner**; the other party is called the **respondent**. The application is started by presenting a document called a petition to the court, which will be initially the County Court. Complex divorces may be transferred to the High Court (Family Division).

The law on divorce is now contained in the Matrimonial Causes Act 1973 as amended by the Matrimonial and Family Proceedings Act 1984. Under these Acts, the **only** ground for divorce is the **irretrievable breakdown** of the marriage. In order to show breakdown, the petitioner must satisfy the court of one or more of the following:

- that the respondent has committed adultery and the petitioner finds it intolerable to live with the respondent
- that the respondent behaved in such a way that the petitioner cannot reasonably be expected to live with the respondent
- desertion by the respondent for two years
- that the husband and wife have lived apart for two years and the respondent consents to the divorce
- that the parties have lived apart for five years.

A petition for divorce cannot be presented unless the parties have been married for a minimum of one year.

It is the duty of both the petitioner's solicitor and of the court to help reconcile the parties. When a person first goes to his or her solicitor, the solicitor should ask whether they have considered reconciliation and will frequently give the client the address of the local Relate clinic, in case this is of assistance. Relate will offer the parties a trained mediator who may be able to help the parties to settle their differences.

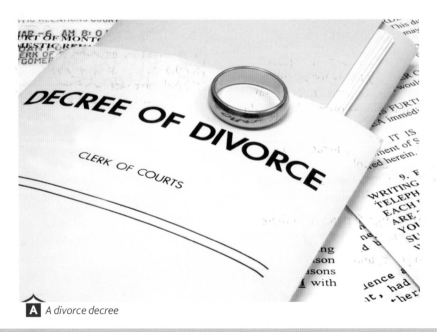

A A divorce decree

B Irretrievable breakdown?

C *Mediation hearing*

Recent proposed changes to the law

Some of the provisions of the Family Law Act 1996 were intended to come into effect by 2000. The aim was to try to save marriages which are regarded as saveable. Therefore certain changes were put forward in the Act.

It was to be compulsory for solicitors to try and effect a reconciliation of the parties, as mentioned above. Couples should be referred to trained mediators, and therefore the divorce would take longer.

The idea of 'no-fault' divorce was introduced, i.e. a divorce could be applied for on proof of irretrievable breakdown without having to prove one of the five 'facts'.

Compulsory **mediation** was piloted in some areas during the late 1990s, but the pilot schemes did not go well. The lack of trained mediators and the parties' unwillingness to participate suggested little benefit had been gained. The Family Law Act 1996 is not now going to be fully implemented.

Divorce procedure

If the Court is to grant the divorce it issues a **decree nisi** at the hearing in favour of the petitioner, but this does not end the marriage. A minimum of six weeks later the petitioner may apply for the decree nisi (which has only ended the marriage provisionally) to be made **absolute** (i.e. final). This involves 'office work', as opposed to another hearing.

A decree absolute will only be issued if satisfactory arrangements have first been made for any children, and as well as the financial arrangements have been sorted out. This is often agreed by the parties with the help of a mediator.

Undefended divorces are normally very straightforward and there is now a provision for divorce by post, where:

- the parties have lived apart for two years, and
- the respondent consents and there are no children; therefore, no public hearing is necessary.

> **Did you know** ??????
>
> The divorce rate in 2007 was the lowest is has been in this country for the last 26 years. Why do you think divorce rates are falling?

■ Maintenance

Maintenance is a financial settlement usually from a husband to maintain a wife and family. It is perfectly possible for a wife to have to pay maintenance to her husband, e.g. where the husband has been awarded custody of the children, or where the wife earns considerably more than the husband. In practice, such awards are rarer.

An order for maintenance may be obtained from the County Court or High Court (Family Division).

The courts may award in addition to a periodical cash payment:

- a lump sum for the spouse and children, or
- a part of the spouse's capital (usually no more than one-third) to be secured for the benefit of the ex-spouse and children
- a transfer of property belonging to the spouse or which was jointly owned.

The Matrimonial Causes Act 1973 s 25, as amended by the Matrimonial and Family Proceedings Act 1984, gives the court a wide discretion regarding maintenance, subject to the following criteria:

- the needs of any children of the marriage are the first priority
- the court should try where possible to work towards a clean break financially between the parties. This is relatively easy where the parties are young or have no young children, less so in other cases.
- the income, earning capacity and financial resources of both parties
- the financial needs and obligations the parties have or are likely to have
- the standard of living enjoyed by the family before the breakdown of the marriage
- the age of the parties and the length of the marriage
- any disability of either party, physical or mental
- the contribution each party made to the welfare of the family
- after a divorce, the value of the loss of some benefit, e.g. a pension, which cannot be acquired because of the divorce
- the conduct of the parties.

The courts have the power to vary the award at any time on the application of either party. The amounts may be increased or reduced or the method of payment varied or the payment stopped, depending on the circumstances, as illustrated by *Cann v Cann* (1977).

One major recent development in this area has been the creation of the Child Support Agency. The aims of the Agency are to ensure that the parents (usually the father) take full responsibility for the maintenance of their children and not simply assume that the State will pick up the bill through increased benefit payments.

The agency has attracted a great deal of criticism in that it appears to be targeting fathers who are already paying some maintenance to make them pay more, and is putting less effort into chasing those fathers who currently pay nothing. There has also been criticism that the agency is completely ignoring so-called 'clean break' settlements between husband and wife, even where that settlement has been approved by a court.

<aside>

Key terms

Maintenance: a financial settlement between the parties.

</aside>

<aside>

Did you know ?????

- The CSA spends 70p of taxpayers' money for every pound it recovers.
- About 300,000 cases are outstanding, with £3.5 billion in payments uncollected since 1993.
- That over half-a-billion pounds have been spent on reforming the CSA in the last 15 years, and MPs still describe the Agency as delivering 'an appalling service'.

</aside>

<aside>

Key case

Cann v Cann (1977)

In 1960, Mrs Cann obtained a separation order and a maintenance order from the Magistrates' Court, and in 1961 the couple were divorced. In 1974, Mrs Cann applied for a variation and maintenance was increased to £7 per week. In 1976, Mr C retired, and applied for a reduction. His weekly income was £23 and Mrs C's was £13. The court reduced the order to £5 per week, i.e. both parties were left with the weekly sum of £18.

</aside>

At the end of 1994, the Government announced a review of the working of the CSA. The review addressed changes to the basis on which spouses are required to pay child maintenance taking into account:

- the financial arrangements on divorce, in particular the nature of any clean break settlement agreed, and
- the financial obligations on divorced spouses who re-marry and acquire new families.

These changes were introduced in 1996, as a result of which the CSA now appears to be operating more fairly. However, there is still an issue with respect to absent fathers who try to avoid making any payments at all and also fathers who pay maintenance but who struggle to get access to their children.

Activities

1 **Criticisms of the law relating to divorce**

You may care to consider the following points. A class debate may be a good way of sorting out the issue and helping you to remember it. Remember, there are no right or wrong answers, but a good discussion always looks at both points of view.

a Should divorce be based on fault, or just the fact that the marriage is over?

b Should mediation be compulsory before a divorce is granted?

c Are the maintenance rules between spouses fair?

d Are the child maintenance rules fair?

2 Which factor is most likely to lead to a divorce? Why do you think that is?

It would be worth sharing your findings with your classmates and discussing the reasons for a higher divorce rate.

Do you think the CSA rules are fair?

Learning summary

You should now be able to:

describe the legal requirement for a divorce and how it is proved

outline the law on maintenance/child maintenance

outline the role of the courts and mediation.

AQA Examiner's tip

The commonest error when describing the law on divorce is to confuse 'irretrievable breakdown' with the 'five facts'. 'Irretrievable breakdown' is the sole **ground** for divorce; the 'five facts' are how irretrievable breakdown can be **proved**.

Make sure you know both the law and process related to divorce. Examination questions always cover both areas.

⬥ links

Find out more about the statistics relating to divorce at: www.statistics.gov.uk/cci/nscl.asp?id=7475

To find out who can apply to the Child Support Agency and how child maintenance is calculated, go to: **www.csa.gov.uk**

Government website on family law: **www.direct.gov.**

Remember

On questions dealing with maintenance, you will need to distinguish between maintenance paid to an ex-spouse and child maintenance paid to support a child of that marriage. The Child Support Agency only deals with the latter.

Intestate succession

Where a person dies without making a valid will, the rules governing who shall be entitled to benefit are governed by the Administration of Estates Act 1925, as amended.

An **administrator**(s) is/are appointed to act for the deceased and to wind up the estate. All property left by the deceased transfers to the administrator upon trust for sale, i.e. **a trust** created for the purpose of selling property for the benefit of the beneficiaries.

The administrator(s) must then pay the debts and funeral expenses of the deceased and distribute the residue in accordance with the intestacy rules.

N.B. Where a beneficiary dies before the intestate his share goes to his issue (children), if he has any.

Comment

There are lots of good reasons for people to make a will. These will be considered in detail later. However, consider that the value of an ordinary family house today may be well over £200,000. If a husband died leaving a wife and children living in a house worth £250,000 the wife would have her husband's personal possessions in the house and then only the interest on half of what was left to live on for the rest of her life (assuming the house was not jointly owned). She may find herself unable to pay any outstanding mortgage, or have very little to actually live on. All this could have been avoided if her husband had left a will making provision for his wife.

Activities

1   Look at the intestacy rules diagram on page 99.

Imagine a husband dies intestate leaving an estate worth £215,000. He leaves a wife, two children, aged 19 and 16, and a brother. How will the intestacy rules apply to his estate? What difference would it make in this situation if he had no children?

2   Look at the article from *The Guardian* newspaper which you will find at: www.guardian.co.uk/money/2005/jun/07/business. willsandinheritancetax

a   Make a note of the key points from the article. You may be able to use them in a discussion question in the examination.

b   One of those points should have been the large number of people who die intestate. Why do you think that is?

c   You could try conducting a survey among family and friends, but be careful not to offend anyone!

A person dies intestate

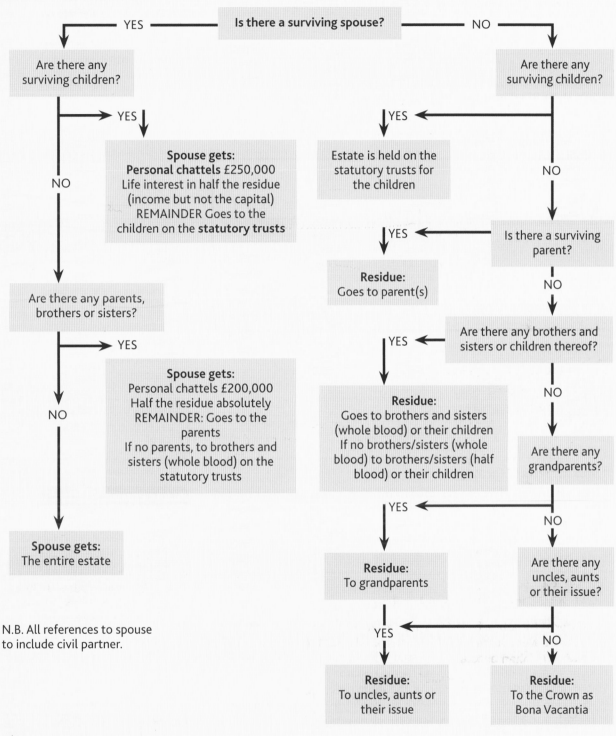

A *What happens when a person dies intestate*

N.B. All references to spouse to include civil partner.

Learning summary

You should now be able to:

describe both the process and the rules when someone dies without leaving a valid will and the requirements of a valid will.

∞links

Key facts on the law of succession:
**www.direct.gov.uk/en/
Governmentcitizensandrights/
Death/Preparation/index.htm**

Testate succession

Capacity to make a will

Any person over 18 and of sound mind may make a valid will. There is one exception to this rule under the Wills (Soldiers and Sailors) Act 1918. Under the Act, a person under 18 years old who is in the Forces on active service may make a will. Also a minor merchant seaman while at sea can make a will. These privileged wills can be informal, i.e. orally with witnesses, or in writing without witnesses.

∞ links

Law Commission website on intestacy and family provision:
www.lawcom.gov.uk/intestate_succession.htm

> **Key case**
>
> ### *Re Jones* (1981)
>
> Jones was a soldier stationed in Northern Ireland. In 1978 he was shot, and on the way to hospital and in front of two officers he said 'If I do not make it, make sure Anne gets all my stuff' (Anne was his fiancée). Jones died the following day.
>
> The court decided that this statement was Jones' last will, even though he had previously made a will in favour of his mother. He was on active military service at this time.

Requirements of a valid will

This is governed by the Wills Act 1837 s 9, re-enacted as Administration of Justice Act 1982 s 17.

No special form is required for a will, but:

- It must be written or typed, but there is no requirement as to what it is written on. The date is not required.
- It must be signed by the **testator** or by someone in his presence and by his direction (initials or a thumb print will do). The signature ought to be at the end of the will. Prior to the new section 17, it was a legal requirement that the testator's signature appeared at the end of the will. This is still desirable, but is no longer a legal requirement, i.e. provisions in the will following the signature may fail, unless it can be proved that the testator intended them to be part of his will, e.g. he signs at the bottom of page 1 and forgets to sign at the bottom of page 2, or he leaves no room to sign at the bottom of page 1 and signs at the top of page 2.
- The will must be properly witnessed. The signature of the testator shall be made or acknowledged by the testator in the presence of two or more witnesses present at the same time, and such witnesses shall sign the will or acknowledge his signature in the presence of the testator. Therefore, there are various possibilities:
  - The most practical would be for the testator and his two witnesses to meet in the same room and then for the testator to sign his will, then for the witnesses to sign their names all at the same time.
  - Alternatively, the testator can sign his will, take it to a room where both the witnesses are at the same time, say 'this is my signature' and then get the two witnesses to sign.

Key terms

Testator: the person who makes a will.

Beneficiary: someone who benefits from an estate under a will.

AQA *Examiner's tip*

Make sure you learn the requirements of a valid will and how to apply them. This is a standard examination question. Revocation and family provision are other popular questions.

AQA *Examiner's tip*

In the examination, draw yourself a family tree of the various people in the scenario. That way you will not miss anyone when dealing with an intestacy.

- The witnesses do not have to see the contents of the will. It is only necessary that they see the testator's signature.
- A person under the age of 18 can witness a will, provided they are old enough to realise the implications of what they are doing, i.e. a 16-year-old should be acceptable but a six-year-old would not.
- A blind person cannot witness a will, because they cannot see the testator's signature (*Re Gibson* (1949)).
- Under the Wills Act 1837, if a **beneficiary** under a will witnesses that will, he will usually lose his bequest, i.e. what he was left under the will, even though the will remains valid.

> **Key case**
>
> ### *Re Bravda* (1968)
>
> The testator made a home-made will and had it properly attested by two witnesses. He then asked his two daughters (sole beneficiaries under the will) to sign it to 'make it stronger'. The court held that, under the 1837 Act, the daughters had to lose their bequests under the will, as they had also witnessed the will.
>
> This case was clearly unfair, and Parliament acted immediately to change the law. Under the Wills Act 1968, provided there are two, independent (not a spouse) witnesses who take no benefit as well as the would-be beneficiary, the beneficiary is allowed to take the benefit. Thus in the above case, the daughters would have kept their bequests, because there were two other witnesses who did not benefit from the will.

> **AQA** *Examiner's tip*
>
> Make sure you know the Intestacy Rules accurately. You can score easy marks in an examination if you can apply the Rules properly. N.B. The calculations always work out easily. If they do not, you have probably made a mistake.

> **Key terms**
>
> **Revocation:** changing or disposing of a will.
>
> **Executor:** personal representative named by the testator.

■ Testate succession

Revocation of a will

A will only takes effect on the death of the testator. Hence a will can be **revoked** or altered at any time up to the testator's death, as follows:

- Another will made later which is inconsistent with the earlier will. Most wills say 'I hereby revoke all former wills …'
- Sometimes a small part of the original will is altered or added to. This can be done by a document called a codicil which is made in the same way as a full will and then kept with it.
- Other writing executed and witnessed as a will, e.g. a letter. The problem here is that, although the letter is likely to have been signed, it is far less likely to have been witnessed.
- Physical destruction, e.g. burning or tearing by, or in the presence of, the testator, and with the intention of revoking the will. If the destruction is accidental, the will remains valid.
- Marriage of the testator after he has made a will. However, a will can be expressly made in contemplation of a particular marriage. This must be stated in the will and the will then remains valid despite the subsequent marriage, provided the testator marries the named person within six months of the will being made.

Divorce does not revoke a will completely, but the ex-spouse is removed as **executor** (if s/he were so appointed) and as beneficiary.

> **Did you know ??????**
>
> Over half a million people died in the UK in 2007. That is not only a lot of funerals, but also a lot of estates to administer. Over half of those people died intestate!

Family provision

Until 1938 a testator had complete freedom of choice to dispose of his estate as he thought fit. He could 'cut out' his wife or a wayward child if he wanted to. The testator can still try to do this but if that person decides to make a claim against the estate of the testator he may be successful. This is known as contesting the will.

The most recent Act on this is the Inheritance (Provision for Family and Dependants) Act 1975. The following people may now claim:

- the spouse
- an ex-spouse who has not remarried
- a child
- any person who was treated by the deceased as a child of the family, e.g. a step-child, adopted child
- any person who immediately before the death of the deceased was being maintained by the deceased, e.g. a mistress, aged relative etc., provided that, either by the deceased's will or the intestacy rules, reasonable financial provision has not been made for them.

This is entirely at the discretion of the court (Chancery Division of the High Court). The court may say that reasonable provision has been made or that in the circumstances the testator was right in not making provision. The reason given by the testator in his will is relevant. The court may order payment of a lump sum and/or periodical payments from the deceased's estate.

Personal representatives

The personal representatives are the people appointed to administer the estate of the deceased on his death.

If a person leaves a will, he will appoint an executor(s). Executors are entitled to act for the deceased when the court grants a document called probate.

If he dies intestate, the court will appoint an administrator(s) by issuing a document called letters of administration.

Money cannot be withdrawn from a bank or a life assurance policy cashed without the personal representative(s) producing either the letters of administration or the grant of probate (unless the estate is worth less than £5,000).

Before the court grants the relevant authority, the personal representatives must prepare a document known as the Inland Revenue affidavit. This lists all the deceased's assets and liabilities. Using this document, an assessment is made for inheritance tax.

Key terms

Family provision: provision which must be made for close family and dependants.

AQA Examiner's tip

If someone acts as both a witness to a will and is also a beneficiary, the will remains valid, but the beneficiary will generally lose their bequest. Many candidates get this wrong in the examination.

Did you know ??????

- During National Will Week, many solicitors will draft your will for free, provided you made a relatively modest donation to a charity of their choice.
- The shortest will ever admitted to probate was just three words long! It said 'All to mother'.

Remember

There are lots of advantages in making a will. How many can you remember without looking?

If you got five or more, you would have no problem with an examination question in that area.

Duties of personal representatives

The personal representatives have a duty to wind up the estate within a year. Within that time they must complete the following:

- **Collect** all the debts owed to the deceased.
- **Pay** all his debts, including funeral expenses, outstanding bills and inheritance tax.
- **Convert** unauthorised investments, e.g. shares, into an authorised investment such as a bank or building society (unless authorised not to by the deceased). This is to protect the value of the estate.
- **Distribute** the remainder of the estate according to either the will or the intestacy rules.

Advantages of making a will

There are many advantages to making a will, as opposed to dying intestate, as follows.

- Complete freedom of choice as to what will happen to one's property on death (subject to the Inheritance (Provision for Family and Dependants) Act 1975).
- The intestacy rules may not be the wishes of the testator, and can change.
- The testator may appoint one or more trusted people (an executor) to deal with his affairs on his death.
- The executor's authority dates from death, whereas it takes time and money for an administrator to be appointed. This delay will cost the estate more money than appointing an executor.
- If a person wishes to be cremated he can state this in his will.
- If a person wishes to make the provision for guardianship of his children, this can be done in a will.
- Sometimes property left can be held in trust. The testator can provide for a specified age greater than 18, e.g. 21 or 25.
- The testator can always change his mind, i.e. alter/revoke his will at any time up to his death.

Activity

1 Look at the Law Commission website at www.lawcom.gov.uk/intestate_succession.htm

a The Law Commission is investigating both the intestacy and family provision rules. How far have they got with the investigation? Discuss in class whether these two sets of rules need reforming and, if so, what changes should be made.

b Follow the link to contact the team working on the report, politely explain that you are a law student and interested in what the Commission is researching. Someone will write back to you, perhaps even with some inside information! You could also do this as a class activity.

Learning summary

You should now be able to:

describe the requirements of a valid will, privileged wills, revocation of a will and the family provision rules

describe the duties of a personal representative

discuss the advantages of making a will.

Chapter summary

8

You should now be able to:

- ✔ explain how to enter into a valid marriage and when a marriage may be either void or voidable
- ✔ explain in outline, the law and legal benefits of civil partnerships
- ✔ explain the law relating to divorce and how divorce cases are proved
- ✔ explain in outline, the law on financial settlements for both ex-spouses and children, following a divorce, including the role of the courts and mediation
- ✔ explain the law of succession, irrespective of whether the deceased has left a valid will or not
- ✔ explain some of the important discussion points relating to family law.

Revision questions

1. What are the prohibited degrees?
2. What is bigamy?
3. What are banns?
4. Name three examples of a marriage that would be void.
5. Name four examples of a marriage that would be voidable.
6. What is the key difference between a void and a voidable marriage?
7. What are the permitted times of marriage?
8. How is a civil partner treated under the intestacy rules?
9. What is the only ground for divorce, and how can that be proved?
10. How long must the parties be married before a divorce petition can be presented?
11. Which court initially handles all divorces?
12. What is Relate?
13. What is the purpose of mediation?
14. What is the key difference between a decree nisi and a decree absolute?
15. Identify five factors which must/can be taken into account before a maintenance order is granted.
16. Which body administers maintenance payments in respect of children?
17. What does intestacy mean and who is appointed to deal with the estate of a person who has died intestate?
18. Identify five advantages of making a will.
19. What are personal chattels?
20. What is meant by a 'life interest'?
21. What are the statutory trusts?
22. When can a person make a privileged will?
23. What are the three requirements of a valid will?
24. Who cannot and who should not witness a will?
25. Identify three ways a will can be partially or completely revoked.
26. Identify four groups of people who can claim under the family provision rules.
27. What is inheritance tax?
28. Identify the four key duties of a personal representative.

9 Rights and responsibilities

What you should already know:

✔ the main classifications of law (Chapter 1)

✔ the structure of courts operating in England and Wales (Chapter 2)

✔ remedies (Chapter 3).

Chapter contents

Buyers and sellers

Employment rights

Rights as a citizen

Introduction to rights and responsibilities

It is often said that we live in a free country, though unlike the United States, we have no Bill of Rights which sets out and protects our various rights and freedoms. Thus, under English law, freedom is defined not as a series of rights but as a range of restrictions. In other words, you can do and say what you want, go where you please, meet who you wish etc. unless in the course of those activities you find yourself legally restricted in some way. The passing of the Human Rights Act 1998 has changed the position somewhat, but not to the extent that it operates as a Bill of Rights as in the US.

It follows that the various rights and freedoms enjoyed by UK citizens cannot be absolute. All rights and freedoms are restricted, either to protect the needs of other citizens or where the needs of the State have to take priority.

In this chapter, we shall be examining three main areas. They are:

1 The rights and responsibilities we have when we enter into a contract, in particular a consumer contract;

2 The rights and responsibilities arising out of a contract of employment; and

3 The rights and responsibilities conferred in certain areas by the Human Rights Act 1998.

9.1 | Buyers and sellers

Buyers and Sellers

Definition of a contract

A contract is a legally binding agreement between two or more parties where both parties have given **consideration**.

Offer

The basis of any contract is the agreement. This means one party (the offeree) agreeing to the **offer** made by the other party (the offeror). Over the years the law has developed a number of rules relating to an offer.

A *Rules on offer*

Rules on offer	Explanation/example
An offer can be made orally, in writing or by conduct	Examples would include: in a shop (oral); buying a house (writing); bidding at an auction (conduct)
An offer can only be accepted by the person, persons or group to whom it is made	An offer can be made to an individual (and can only be accepted by that individual)
	An offer can be made to a group of people (and can only be accepted within that group)
	An offer can be made, through advertising, to the whole world (and can be accepted by anyone)
An offer must be communicated	You cannot accept an offer you know nothing about
An offer must be distinguished from an **invitation to treat**	An invitation to treat is an invitation by one party to do business – i.e. 'make me an offer'. The important point is that an invitation to treat cannot be accepted, whereas an offer can

Termination (ending) of an offer

When an offer has terminated, it cannot be accepted by the offeree and therefore there cannot be a contract.

Key case

Offer and acceptance – Carlill v Carbolic Smoke Ball Co (1893)

The defendant company advertised that it would give £100 to anyone who caught flu after having used their smokeball as prescribed. Mrs Carlill complied with the advert and instructions, caught flu and sued for the money when the company refused to pay. The company argued that you cannot make an offer to the whole world, and that Mrs C had not communicated her acceptance of the offer.

The court decided that:

1 You can make an offer to the whole world through advertising

2 Mrs C did not need to communicate her acceptance – complying with the advert was enough.

Therefore, she won the case.

An offer may come to an end in one of five ways:

B *Termination*

Rules on termination of offer	Explanation/example
Rejection or refusal	The offeree simply says no to the offer
Counter-offer	This is where the offeree does not accept the original offer but makes an offer of his own. In such a case the original offer is terminated
Revocation	An offeror can revoke (i.e. take back) his offer provided he communicates the revocation to the offeree before **acceptance**
Lapse of time	If the offeror sets a time limit, then the offer will end when that time limit runs out. If no time limit is specified, then the offer must be accepted within a reasonable time. What is reasonable will depend on the circumstances E.g. an offer to sell perishable goods must be accepted quickly, but with more durable goods a longer period would be reasonable
Death	If either the offeror or the offeree dies before acceptance, then the offer will end

AQA **Examiner's tip**

Learn the basic rules of offer and acceptance carefully and practise applying them. Your teacher will give you examples or you can use AQA's GCSE Law past papers. Candidates in an exam often know the rules but are not as confident in applying them.

Invitation to treat – *Fisher* v *Bell* (1960)

Key case

Under the Restriction of Offensive Weapons Act 1959 it was an offence to offer for sale certain classes of weapons including flick-knives. The defendant had a flick-knife in his shop window with a price ticket on it. A policeman saw this, entered the shop and arrested the defendant, who was charged under the Act. The court decided that he was not guilty. The display was an invitation to treat, not an offer to sell.

Offer and acceptance, counter-offers – *Hyde* v *Wrench* (1840)

Key case

Wrench offered to sell a farm to Hyde for £1,000. Hyde offered £950, which Wrench refused. Hyde then tried to accept the original offer of £1,000 but Wrench refused to sell. Hyde sued Wrench for breach of contract and failed. The original offer had been rejected and was destroyed by the counter-offer and could not be revived. Wrench was therefore entitled to reject Hyde's new offer.

Revocation – *Payne* v *Cave* (1789)

Key case

Cave, at an auction, made a bid for Payne's goods. Before the fall of the hammer, Cave shouted out and withdrew his bid. Nevertheless the goods were knocked down to Cave who refused to pay. Payne sued Cave for breach of contract. Payne's claim failed because Cave had clearly revoked his offer before the hammer fell.

Acceptance

Acceptance occurs when the offeree agrees to all the terms of the offer, thereby turning the offer into a contract. Just as with offer, there are a number of rules relating to acceptance.

C *Rules on acceptance*

Rules on acceptance	Explanation/example
Acceptance must be communicated to the offeror	This may be done either orally or in writing. If there is no communication, then there will be no acceptance
	An exception to this rule is a unilateral contract, e.g. a reward case. Remember *Carlill* v *Carbolic Smoke Ball Co* (1893). In such a situation, acceptance is implied from the conduct of the acceptor
The **postal rule**	This is an exception to the rule that acceptance must be communicated to the offeror
	If the offeror is prepared to accept an acceptance by post, then the offer is accepted as soon as the letter is posted, regardless of whether or not the offeror receives it, but:
	a the acceptance must be posted correctly; i.e. it must be stamped, sealed, correctly addressed and placed in the post-box. Handing it to the postman will not suffice
	b the postal rule only applies to acceptance. A letter containing either an offer or a revocation must actually be received by the offeree to have legal effect
Acceptance must be unqualified	The offeree can only accept the offer as it was made and not add any conditions or terms

Communication of acceptance – Felthouse v Bindley (1862)

Felthouse offered to buy his nephew's horse for £30. He wrote 'If I hear no more about him, I shall consider the horse mine at £30.' The nephew did not reply, but he did ask Bindley, an auctioneer, not to sell the horse as he had sold it to his uncle. In error, Bindley sold the horse to someone else and Felthouse sued Bindley. Felthouse's claim failed because the horse did not belong to him. The nephew had not communicated his acceptance to his uncle.

Nature of acceptance – Neale v Merritt (1930)

Merritt offered to sell land to Neale for £280. Neale replied, accepting and enclosed a cheque for £80, promising to pay the balance by four £50 instalments. Merritt refused to proceed and Neale sued for breach. Neale's action failed because his 'acceptance' was not exactly the same as Merritt's offer.

■ Consumer protection

This area of law is governed by three main Acts of Parliament.

Sale of Goods Act 1979

A contract for the sale of goods is where goods are exchanged for money. Under the Act, certain **implied terms** (not stated) are included in the contract, in addition to any terms which the parties have agreed. These implied terms are as follows.

Postal rule – Household Fire Insurance Co v Grant (1879)

Grant applied for shares in the company. A letter accepting Grant's application was posted to Grant, but never reached him. Grant refused to pay and was sued by Household Fire Insurance Co. The court decided that Grant was liable because the contract was complete when the letter of acceptance was posted.

Instantaneous forms of communication – Entores Ltd v Miles Far East Corporation (1955)

A London-based company sent an offer by telex (a teleprinter machine) to an Amsterdam-based company. The acceptance was also by telex. A dispute arose and the court had to decide whether to apply English or Dutch law. (If acceptance was completed when the telex was sent – Dutch law; if when it was received – English law.) The court decided that English law applied because that was where the acceptance was received. The postal rule does not apply to instantaneous means of communication.

Postal rule: the contract is complete as soon as the letter of acceptance is posted.

Implied term: a promise in a contract, not discussed by the parties.

Satisfactory quality: the standard of goods one would expect to receive.

Fitness for purpose: goods able to do what is promised.

Sales by sample: inspect a small quantity and buy a large quantity.

Product: manufactured goods.

D *Implied terms under the Sale of Goods Act 1979 (as amended)*

Section Implied term	Explanation	Case
Section 12 **Right to sell**	Under s 12(1), the seller implies that he has the right to sell the goods Under s 12(2), there is an implied term that the goods shall be free from third party rights and that the buyer shall enjoy quiet (*undisturbed*) possession	*Rowland* v *Divall* (1923) Rowland bought a car from Divall, who had stolen it from the true owner. Thus Rowland was bound to return the car to the true owner, and Rowland successfully sued Divall for the full price he had paid
Section 13 **Sale by description**	Section 13 states that where goods are sold by description, they must correspond with that description Sales over the counter, even in self-service stores, are still sales by description because most goods are described only by the package in which they are contained, e.g. a tin of baked beans A buyer will succeed under s 13 even if he has seen and examined the goods, providing the discrepancy between the description and reality could not reasonably have been discovered by such an examination. This is illustrated in *Beale* v *Taylor* (1967)	*Beale* v *Taylor* (1967) Taylor advertised a car for sale as a '1961 Triumph Herald 1200'. Beale inspected the car. On the car was a metal disc with the figures 1200 on it. Beale bought the car, but later found that the car was the rear of a 1961 Triumph Herald 1200 welded to the front of an earlier Triumph Herald 948. Beale sued for damages under s 13 and was awarded a full refund
Section 14(2) **as amended by the Sale and Supply of Goods Act 1994** **Satisfactory Quality**	Under s 14(2), where the seller sells goods in the course of a business (excludes private sales) the goods shall be of **satisfactory quality** except (i) as regards any defects drawn to the buyer's attention (ii) when the buyer examines the goods and ought to have seen any defects. Satisfactory quality is judged based on both the **description** and **price** of the goods and (under the 1994 Act) **appearance and finish**, **durability**, **safety** and **freedom from minor defects**	*Wilson* v *Rickett Cockerell* (1954) A housewife, Mrs Wilson, was injured by the explosion of a detonator delivered in a sack of Coalite. The Court of Appeal said that the consignment as a whole was not of merchantable (now satisfactory) quality, and therefore Mrs Wilson was entitled to damages
Section 14(3) **Fitness for purpose**	Under s 14(3), where the seller sells goods in the course of a business (excludes private sales) and the buyer expressly, or by implication, makes known to the seller any particular purpose for which the goods are being bought, there is an implied condition that the goods supplied under the contract are reasonably **fit for that purpose** Where the buyer does not make known the purpose for which he requires the goods in question, then the goods must be fit for the 'usual and obvious purpose'	*Kendall* v *Lillico* (1969) Brazilian ground nut extraction was sold in order that it could be made into foodstuff for cattle and poultry. All the turkeys fed on the extraction died The court decided that there was a clear breach of s 14(3) as the food was unfit for feeding to poultry *Priest* v *Last* (1903) Priest purchased a hot water bottle from Last, but did not state why he wanted it. The bottle burst on the fifth time of using, having been filled with hot water The court decided that the bottle was not fit for the usual and obvious purpose of filling with hot water and therefore Last was in breach of s 14(3). Damages were awarded
Section 15 **Sales by sample** **Section 15(2) (a), (b), (c)**	(a) the bulk must correspond (exactly) with the sample in quality, and (b) the buyer shall have a reasonable opportunity to compare the bulk with the sample, and (c) the goods shall be free of any defect rendering them unsatisfactory and which would not be apparent on reasonable examination of the sample	*Ruben Ltd* v *Faire Bros Ltd* (1949) The sellers agreed to supply the buyers with a quantity of 'Linatex' (sheets of rubber) in 41 ft rolls, 5 ft wide, in accordance with a small sample. The sample was flat and soft, but the rubber delivered was crinkly and folded. The buyers refused to accept delivery and were sued by the sellers. It was decided that the **product** supplied was not exactly in accordance with the sample and therefore the sellers were in breach of s 15(2)(a)

Sale of goods – Godley v Perry and others (1960)

Perry, a retailer, purchased from a wholesaler a quantity of toy catapults, the sale being by sample. One of them was sold to Godley, a small boy, who injured his eye when it broke into pieces because of faulty construction. Perry had to pay damages to the boy and claimed that money back from the wholesaler. The defect in the catapult had not been discovered by the retailer when he pulled back the elastic of the catapult in his shop. The court decided that Perry was liable to Godley under s 14 (2) because the catapult was not of merchantable (satisfactory) quality. The wholesaler was found liable under s 15 (2)(c) because the catapults contained a hidden defect which Perry could not reasonably have discovered when he tested the sample in the shop. Therefore the wholesaler had to refund the damages which Perry had paid to Godley.

1 Log on to the Consumer Direct website using the link at the beginning of this Chapter.

a Make a list of ten useful tips from the various links available. Put those tips in order of how useful they may be.

b Explain to your classmates why you chose those ten useful tips and why you put them in the order you did.

c Produce a list of the ten best tips from the entire class.

Supply of Goods and Services Act 1982

The Supply of Goods and Services Act 1982 is designed to protect the consumer of services, as opposed to goods, e.g. car repairs, meals in a restaurant, etc. Where the contract involves goods and services, then the appropriate law will apply to the different elements of the contract. Therefore a garage fitting a new engine will be liable for the engine under the 1979 Act and the labour under the 1982 Act. This Act also includes terms which are implied into a contract for the provision of services.

E *Care and skill, time and price*

Section Implied term	Explanation	Case/example
Section 13 Care and skill	There is an implied term that the supplier will carry out his service with reasonable care and skill	A garage mechanic who negligently forgets to tighten the wheel nuts so the wheel falls off, thereby causing damage to the vehicle and/or injury to the owner, will make his employer liable under the Act
Section 14 Time	Where the contract is silent on time, there is an implied term that the supplier will carry out his service within a reasonable time. The case opposite is pre-Act but would be decided exactly the same today	*Charnock* v *Liverpool Corporation* (1968) Liverpool Corporation took a car to Charnock's garage for repair. No delivery date was agreed and the repairs took eight weeks. The corporation sued for damages on the basis that the repairs had taken an unreasonable amount of time, and the claim succeeded
Section 15 Price	Where the contract is silent on price, there is an implied term that the consumer will pay a reasonable charge. This provision will apply in particular to estimates, where the final bill is considerably higher than the original estimate. The section will not apply to quotations, as these have to be accurate anyway	A bathroom company estimate the cost of a complete new bathroom at £4,000. If the final bill is £4,200 that would probably be reasonable. If the final bill was £6,000 that would be unreasonable If the company had quoted £4,000, that is all the customer has to pay

◼ Consumer Protection Act 1987

This Act was passed as a direct result of EEC Directive 85/374 of July 1985 to harmonise the law of the member states on liability for defective products. In effect it is an extension to the law of negligence which imposes strict liability on the manufacturer of a defective product instead of the claimant having to prove the usual elements of duty of care, breach and damage (see Chapter 6). The law under the 1987 Act is explained in the following table.

F *Consumer Protection Act 1987*

Principle	Explanation
Basic liability	**Section 2(1)** of the Act imposes liability for damage caused by a defective product. The word 'product' implies a manufacturing process. Thus a bottle of ginger beer would fall within the Act, unprocessed fruit and vegetables would not
Persons who may be liable	The Act imposes liability on the producer of a product, usually therefore the manufacturer. However, an 'own-brander' also falls within the definition of a producer. This is a common practice in supermarkets where food/drink is sold under the supermarket's own name. In this case, it is the supermarket that would be liable under the 1987 Act, not whoever manufactured the item for the store
Defect	**Section 3(1)** states that there is a defect in a product 'if the safety of the product is not such as persons generally are entitled to expect.' The following factors may be relevant: The purposes for which the product has been manufactured, i.e. has the product been used for its intended purpose? The effectiveness of any warnings supplied with the product, e.g. a bottle of bleach or a firework The adequacy of the instructions, e.g. 'light the blue touch paper and retire
Damage	'Damage' is defined by **section 5(1)** to include death, personal injury or loss of or damage to property. This wide definition is limited in two ways: It does not include damage to the product itself. This would be covered under the Sale of Goods Act and the retailer would be liable It does not include claims where the damage is less than £275. This was our government, perhaps unfairly, excluding 'minor' claims
Defences	That the product was not defective under s 3 That the claimant was entirely or partly at fault in the way the product was used, e.g. ignoring clear instructions/warnings That the product did not cause the damage That more than three years has elapsed since the right to claim arose That more than ten years has elapsed since the product first appeared on the market That 'The state of scientific and technical knowledge at the time when he put the product into circulation was not such as to enable the existence of the defect to be discovered.' Effectively the producer is claiming that nothing he could have done could have prevented the defect in the product

Remember

Enforcement procedures through the small claims track of the county court are an important part of consumer protection. It is no good having rights and no understanding of how to enforce them. The details of how the small claims process operates are in Chapter 3.

Did you know ??????

You have more rights if you buy something on a credit card than if you pay by cash or debit card. You can find out why by going to the Consumer Direct website.

Learning summary

You should now be able to:

outline and apply the law of contract, in particular the law on offer and acceptance

describe and apply the law on consumer protection

outline and apply the law on enforcement through small claims

demonstrate an outline critical awareness of the law relating to buyers and sellers.

9.2 Employment rights

Employment law

The relationship between employer and employee is based on a contract. With the majority of contracts, the parties are free to make their own bargain. This is less apparent in contracts of employment, due initially to collective bargaining agreements between employers and trade unions and in more recent times due to a succession of Acts of Parliament.

Form of the contract

As with other contracts, contracts of employment may be made by word of mouth. However, the Employment Rights Act 1996 (as amended) provides that an employer must give all employees a written statement of the main terms of their contract of employment within two months of starting work. This statement must include the following:

- name of employer and employee
- date of starting work
- job title
- rates of pay and method and interval of payment
- hours of work
- holiday entitlement and holiday pay
- sickness, injury and sick pay provisions
- pension entitlements
- notice requirements
- grievance and disciplinary procedures.

Duties of the employer and employee

These duties are set out in the table below.

A Duties of an employer

Duties of an employer	Duties of an employee
To pay wages as agreed It is up to the employer to choose the method of payment, but an itemised pay statement must be provided. Rates of pay are negotiable, but cannot fall below the national minimum wage, introduced in 1999	**To exercise reasonable care and skill** For example, not to damage the employer's property
References There is no legal duty for an employer to give a reference to an ex-employee, but if one is given, the reference is subject to the law of defamation (see 9.3)	**To obey all reasonable instructions** Failure to do so may be a breach of contract, and may be a ground for dismissal
To indemnify against liability and loss This is known as **vicarious liability** and was mentioned in Chapter 6 and will be developed later in this chapter	**To be loyal and faithful** E.g. not to give away trade secrets or confidential information
To provide a safe system of work This area is now governed by the Health and Safety at Work Act 1974	**To comply with the Health and Safety at Work Act 1974**
Not to discriminate against employees	

Vicarious liability

Providing the employee is acting within the **course of his employment**, the employer will be responsible for any loss incurred by the employee. This principle is known as **vicarious liability**. Vicarious liability most often occurs when an employee is sued for negligence.

The difference between an employee and an independent contractor

An employer is not generally responsible for the torts of an independent contractor. The difference between an employee and an independent contractor is therefore very important in law. Usually an employee is employed under a contract of service and therefore is told what to do and how to do it. Thus his employer exercises control over his employee's actions and will be vicariously responsible for those actions. An independent contractor will be told what to do, but how he does it is generally up to him. Therefore the independent contractor will usually be responsible for his own torts.

The arguments for vicarious liability

The principle of vicarious liability can be justified on a number of grounds:

■ Employees are working for the employer's profit; therefore it is only fair that the employer should also run the risk of any losses.

■ The injured claimant would rather sue an employer with resources than a potential 'man of straw' employee.

■ Employers must be insured; employees need not be.

Health and Safety at Work Act 1974

As we have seen, this Act applies to both employer and employee and creates duties which both must comply with. The main provisions of the Act are as follows.

The employer must with respect to his employees:

■ maintain the health and safety at work of his employees

■ maintain a safe system of work

■ maintain a safe method of handling, storing and transporting various articles and substances

■ provide adequate instruction, supervision and training to his employees.

The employer must with respect to the general public:

■ conduct the business in such a way so as not to expose the public to risks which may be dangerous to their health and safety.

The employee must:

■ take reasonable care for the health and safety of himself/others at work

■ cooperate with the provisions of the Act.

The Act is enforced by the Health and Safety Commission and Executive; both bodies were set up by the Act. Inspectors appointed by the Executive have powers to enter premises and make investigations.

Key terms

Course of employment: an employee who is at work and doing his job.

Vicarious liability: an employer's responsibility for the actions of an employee.

∞ links

Free access to the key principles dealing with employment law: **www.emplaw.co.uk**

A website with a range of cases on the operation of the Equal Pay Act 1970: **www.equalityni.org/archive/word/Aug04Casestudiesequalpay.doc**

Beard v *London General Omnibus Co* (1900)

A bus conductor, employed by London General Omnibus Co (LGO), drove a bus in London and negligently collided with Beard. Beard sued LGO in the tort of negligence. The court decided that Beard's claim against the employer must fail because a bus conductor is employed to collect fares, not drive the bus.

Key case

They may issue a prohibition notice (an order commanding a particular activity to cease) or an improvement notice (an order commanding a particular activity to be improved as regards health and safety). Failure to comply with either notice can lead to the employer being prosecuted which may mean a heavy fine or even a prison sentence.

Discrimination in employment

There are three principal Acts of Parliament with respect to **discrimination** in employment. These are:

- Race Relations Act 1976
- Sex Discrimination Act 1975
- Equal Pay Act 1970
- Disability Discrimination Act 2005.

Race Relations Act 1976

This makes it unlawful to discriminate against a person on racial grounds (i.e. on grounds of colour, race or nationality). The Act applies equally to employers and potential employers. It also applies in other areas, such as housing, education, access to certain facilities and services etc.

Any person who believes he has been discriminated against on racial grounds in the employment field may complain to an employment **tribunal** who may award compensation, or may order the guilty party to remove or reduce the effects of the discrimination. Furthermore, the Commission for Racial Equality, set up under the Act, can make investigations of alleged discrimination and order a guilty party to stop.

Sex Discrimination Act 1975

This makes it unlawful for employers to discriminate against a person (male or female) on the grounds of sex when it comes to advertising, engaging, promoting or training, e.g. advertising for a male shop assistant or teacher would be unlawful. There are some minor exceptions, e.g. it would not be unlawful to advertise for a female attendant in a ladies changing room on the grounds of modesty!

Any person who believes he/she has been discriminated against on the ground of sex has the right to complain to an employment tribunal. In addition, the Equal Opportunities Commission, created by the 1975 Act, is charged with enforcing the 1970 and 1975 Acts and promoting equality of opportunity between the sexes generally.

Equal Pay Act 1970

This supplements the provisions of the 1975 Act. It covers such details as rates of pay, holiday and sick pay, working hours, and provides that a woman must not be treated less favourably than a male colleague doing the same or a similar or equivalent job. Equal Pay Act cases can be found via the link on page 113.

Key case

Dexter v Tenby Electrical Accessories Ltd (1990)

Tenby occupied a factory and engaged an independent contractor to work on the factory roof. An employee of the contractor fell through the roof, which was shown to be unsafe. Tenby was prosecuted for the safety breach. The court decided that the company was guilty of the breach, even where the injured party was employed by someone else.

Key terms

Discrimination: treating someone unfairly because of their race, gender or disability.

Tribunal: a body which deals with disputes in employment.

Key case

Garland v British Rail Engineering Ltd (1979)

British Rail Engineering Ltd (BR) provided free travel for the spouse and children of all its employees. When a male employee retired, BR continued to provide free travel for his wife and children, but when a female employee retired the privilege was withdrawn from her family. Garland, a female who was still employed by BR, claimed these arrangements were contrary to the Sex Discrimination Act 1975. The case eventually went to the European Court of Justice, where it was decided that BR were operating a travel policy in breach of the Sex Discrimination Act.

Remember

If you learn the table of differences between the duties of employers and employees you will have a clear understanding of the requirements of this part of the Law specification.

Disability Discrimination Acts 1995 and 2005

These Acts are intended to give disabled people significantly greater rights in the area of employment. The Acts prohibit discrimination in relation to employment of disabled people, including recruitment, training, promotion, benefits, dismissal, etc. The 1995 Act also requires employers to make reasonable adjustments for a disabled person put at a substantial disadvantage by either a way of working or the physical nature of the workplace. Someone who is a victim of disability discrimination can apply for damages before an employment tribunal.

■ Enforcement of employee rights

Employees have a range of rights with respect to their employer, e.g. in relation to their contract, dismissal, redundancy, maternity, discrimination etc.

Tribunals

A tribunal is a body set up outside the normal court structure to deal with a range of disputes. They have become increasingly common since the late 1940s, and have helped considerably in relieving the burden on the ordinary civil court structure. Tribunals operate much more informally than the courts, and this has the benefit of allowing ordinary people to present their own cases in a reasonably unintimidating atmosphere. Tribunals are also much quicker and cheaper than the civil courts. However there are also disadvantages. Legal representation is not available, and appeals are only available on a limited basis.

An employee who believes that their rights have been infringed has the right to complain to an employment tribunal. The application to the tribunal must generally be made within three months of the cause of complaint. A person who wishes to appeal against an employment tribunal decision has a right of appeal to the employment appeal tribunal and from there to the Court of Appeal and beyond. An example of such a case is *Garland* v *British Rail Engineering* (1979) on the previous page.

Activity

1 Log on to the Tribunal Service website: www.employmenttribunals.gov.uk

By following the links, you will be able to find out where the nearest employment tribunal is to where you live. You should also be able to access a range of free publications, the range of cases this tribunal deals with and also how tribunals work in terms of making a claim.

a Compare this information to what you learnt about civil procedure in Chapter 3. Make a list of the advantages and disadvantages of suing someone through the civil courts as opposed to the advantages and disadvantages of making a claim through an employment tribunal.

b Compare your list with those produced by your classmates. Can you all agree on common advantages and disadvantages?

Learning summary

You should now be able to:

demonstrate an outline understanding of the nature of the contract between employers and employees

demonstrate an outline understanding of the principle of vicarious liability

describe and apply the key provisions of the Health and Safety at Work Act 1974

describe and apply the range of discrimination laws in employment

demonstrate an outline critical awareness of employment law.

AQA Examiner's tip

The following are common student errors which you can try and avoid:

■ not understanding the difference between an employee and an independent contractor

■ forgetting that a breach of the Health and Safety at Work Act leads to a criminal prosecution

■ not supporting answers on discrimination with relevant authority (Act or case).

Rights and responsibilities as a citizen (human rights)

Opinion will vary when considering which basic rights every human being should be entitled to. Most people would consider the right to life and personal freedom (liberty) to be priorities; but what other rights should human beings have, purely because they are human beings?

Activity

1 Human rights

a Discuss with the person next to you what rights you think every human being should have and why.

b When you have done this, compare your lists to the rights and freedoms protected by law, in Table **A**.

You may find that you did not even mention some of the fundamental rights in law, as you took them for granted, concentrating on higher level rights. This shows you live in a free society! Not everyone in the world would think this way, because they have experienced serious violations of their fundamental human rights.

The European Convention on Human Rights 1950

To encourage unity among the European nations following the Second World War, governments in the Council of Europe made an agreement that all citizens in their countries would be allowed certain rights, which they considered to be the 'foundation of justice and peace in the world.'

This agreement was called the European Convention on Human Rights. Further agreements, called 'protocols', added more rights and freedoms.

The European Court of Human Rights

As the Convention does not have legal effect in the UK, the UK courts did not have the power to rule that UK laws were incompatible with human rights. As a result, cases had to be brought to the European Court of Human Rights in Strasbourg (NE France). This made it a long and expensive process.

The Human Rights Act 1998

The Human Rights Act came into force in October 2000, outlining the Convention rights in an Act of Parliament. This made those rights enforceable in the UK courts. The Act states Parliament's intention that all UK laws and **public bodies** will comply with the Convention. So now the UK courts have the power to declare that any UK law or policy is incompatible with Convention rights. This may avoid the need for the case to be decided by the European Court of Human Rights (although this is still possible if the case is unsuccessful in the UK courts).

Objectives

In this topic you will learn:

how to demonstrate an outline understanding of the Human Rights Act 1998 and the European Convention on Human Rights

how to demonstrate an understanding of rights and restrictions in relation to personal freedom, freedom of expression and the right to a fair trial.

Did you know ??????

Cases concerning the European Convention on Human Rights are heard in the European Court of Human Rights (in Strasbourg), but cases concerning European law (made by the European institutions) are heard in the European Court of Justice (in Luxembourg).

Key terms

Public bodies: any organisation serving a government purpose or public function, e.g. local authorities, the courts, police service, prison service, etc.

∞ links

For further details on the rights and restrictions in the European Convention on Human Rights go to the website of the European Court of Human Rights: **www.echr.coe.int/echr**

Under the heading 'English' Click 'basic texts' then click 'English'.

A *European Convention on Human Rights made in Rome 1950*

Article	Right/freedom
1	All countries whose governments sign up to the agreement will grant their citizens these rights
2	The right to life (Protocol 13 abolishes the death penalty)
3	The right to be free from torture or inhuman or degrading treatment or punishment
4	The right to be free from slavery
5	The right to liberty and security of the person (personal freedom)
6	The right to a fair and public hearing within a reasonable time by an independent and impartial tribunal established by law (the right to a fair trial)
7	The right not to be convicted of a crime which was not a crime when the act was committed
8	The right to respect for private and family life, home and correspondence
9	The right to freedom of thought, conscience or religion
10	The right to freedom of expression (commonly called freedom of speech)
11	The right to freedom of peaceful assembly and association (to meet with others or join organisations)
12	The right to marry and establish a family
13	The right to a remedy if these rights are not granted
14	The right to be free from discrimination in relation to these rights
Protocols 1 and 4 Made in Paris 1952 and Strasbourg 1963	The right to peaceful enjoyment of possessions The right to education The right to secret, free voting in elections at regular intervals The right to choose where to live if lawfully in that country; to leave a country; to stay in a country of which a person is a national

This has not abolished **Parliamentary supremacy**, however, as Parliament is entitled to ignore a declaration of incompatibility from the courts if they choose to. They could even pass a new Act abolishing the Human Rights Act (although they would have to consider carefully the impact of this decision).

The Human Rights Act states that all new Acts of Parliament must contain a statement that they are either compatible with the Human Rights Act or that they are not, but that Parliament wishes to proceed anyway. It also states that judges should interpret all law in a way that upholds these rights.

Key rights – restrictions and protection

Few rights are *absolute* rights, which can never be restricted by law, such as the right to freedom from torture. Most rights may be limited by law in specific circumstances, to meet a legitimate aim. Rights of individuals must be balanced against the needs of the wider community or the country as a whole.

∞ links

See Chapter 5 for information on Acts of Parliament.

For more information regarding human rights go to **www.direct.gov.uk/en/ Governmentcitizensandrights**

See Chapter 2 for details of what constitutes a lawful arrest; the law regarding bail and custodial sentences.

See Topic 6.3 for details of the tort of trespass to the person and to land.

Key terms

Parliamentary supremacy (human rights): the theory that all types of law are less important than Acts of Parliament and that Parliament can make any law it chooses.

1 Personal freedom (right to liberty and security)

This is the freedom to go where you want to go and not to be deprived of your liberty. There are many ways this freedom may be restricted by law, including:

Criminal law restrictions

- A lawful arrest (by police or other citizens). If an arrest is unlawful it may lead to a false imprisonment case in the civil courts, as it is a trespass to the person.
- The decision to refuse bail and remand a person in custody pending a criminal trial or conditions placed on bail.
- A custodial sentence given following a criminal trial.

Civil law restrictions

- Detention under the Mental Health Act 1983 (as amended) of those who are mentally disordered.
- The law of trespass to land prevents people from entering land without permission.

2 Freedom of expression (communication/speech)

- This is commonly called 'freedom of speech' but it covers all forms of communication, not just the spoken word, including any method of giving or receiving ideas or information. This includes gestures, drawings, performances, the written word, illustrations, dances, plays and films. In a free society, the ability of citizens to speak their minds on important issues, even if this means criticising the government, is crucial. This freedom is, however, restricted in a variety of ways by law, including:

Criminal law restrictions

- If a person has agreed to abide by The Official Secrets Acts 1911 and 1989, they are prevented from communicating certain information, gained while working for a public body, which may be 'damaging' to public safety.
- Under the Obscene Publications Act 1959, obscene communications through literature or art, including arts such as plays and films, are prohibited. This is defined as anything a person may see, hear or read which may 'deprave or corrupt a significant proportion' of its likely audience.
- Common law prevents blasphemy and blasphemous libel through attacks on the Church of England and Christianity. This does not apply to other religions.
- The Public Order Act 1986 makes it a criminal offence to incite racial hatred.

Civil law restriction

- The tort of defamation prevents people from lowering another's reputation by publishing untrue statements.

3 Right to a fair trial

The right to a fair trial by an impartial court is fundamental in a free society. This right is protected in many ways by law, including:

- The availability of public funding (formerly called legal aid). This will pay for legal advice and representation in serious criminal

Try to remember whether a restriction on a freedom is a civil or a criminal law restriction. If you find it difficult to remember these restrictions in the exam – think logically about why people can't go wherever they like; why they can't say what they like and what makes trials in the UK courts fair.

Key case

Monson v *Tussauds* (1894)

A waxwork of Monson was placed near figures of convicted murderers in Madame Tussauds. Monson had been tried for murder, but not convicted. He sued for libel, and his claim succeeded.

Byrne v *Deane* (1937)

A golf club had an illegal gambling machine in the clubhouse. Someone informed the police, who removed the machine. A poem appeared on the golf club notice board which suggested that the informant was Byrne, who sued the writer for defamation. His claim failed because 'right-thinking members of society' would approve of informing the police of an illegal activity, not think worse of the informer.

∞ links

See Chapter 4 for details of duty solicitors and for details of lay people (magistrates and juries).

cases, by solicitors and barristers who have a contract to provide those services on behalf of the Community Legal Service.

- The courts must abide by the 'rule of law' and rules of 'natural justice'. The rule of law means that nobody is above the law and everybody (except the Queen) is subject to normal legal processes if suspected of breaking the law. The rules of natural justice mean that in all courts both sides must have the opportunity to be heard by an unbiased person, acting in good faith and the opportunity to examine each other's witnesses.

- The verdict in virtually all criminal cases is decided by a group of lay people (exception district judges – see Chapter 4). This allows a defendant to be judged by their peers rather than being arrested, charged, tried and sentenced by paid representatives of the state.

- A defendant in a criminal trial is innocent until proven guilty. To be convicted, the prosecution must make the magistrates or jury 'sure of' the defendant's guilt – this is what 'beyond reasonable doubt' means.

- A structured appeals system, which allows people to challenge decisions made by the courts.

Many would argue that human rights are under attack at an unprecedented rate in recent years, largely due to measures designed to counteract terrorist threats. Most would agree that a truly free society should restrict basic rights only where an impartial court has decided that this is in the best interests of that society.

Activity

2   In the following situations, name the freedom involved; the restriction or protection placed on it and whether this is a civil or criminal restriction, if appropriate.

a   Zac believes that testing products on animals is wrong, so he distributes leaflets which say that Professor Smith, from the local animal testing centre, is a criminal.

b   Yvette is a member of a community group who are annoyed because of the influx of immigrant workers into their area. She produces posters which make false claims against them and to encourage the community not to serve them in their shops or employ them in their businesses.

c   William kicks his ball into his neighbour's back garden. He knows they are at work and that they have banned him from going into their garden, but he climbs over the fence to get his ball back.

d   Vivien has been arrested for punching Ulrica in a fight, breaking her nose. She cannot afford to pay for legal advice as she is on a low income. She has been told she may have to stay in custody until her trial.

e   Tim works for a government department and he finds out that the government are holding talks with another state over environmental issues. He calls Greenpeace to let them know the proposals.

f   Susan is on a jury in a criminal trial. She thinks that the defendant may be innocent but feels like she has to agree with the other jurors.

Learning summary

You should now be able to:

demonstrate an outline understanding of the Human Rights Act 1998 and the European Convention on Human Rights

demonstrate an understanding of rights and restrictions in relation to personal freedom, freedom of expression and the right to a fair trial.

9

You should now be able to:

✔ know that, in law, rights are balanced by corresponding duties and that rights are generally restricted by the law

✔ demonstrate an understanding of the rights and responsibilities involved in contract law with particular emphasis on consumer law

✔ demonstrate an understanding of the rights and responsibilities involved in a contract of employment

✔ demonstrate an understanding of the rights and responsibilities of citizenship

✔ demonstrate an outline critical awareness of the notion of rights and responsibilities, with particular emphasis on the areas of law indicated above.

Revision questions

1. What is the definition of a contract and what are the key elements within that definition?

2. How can an offer be made?

3. Why must an offer be communicated?

4. What is an invitation to treat?

5. What is a counter-offer?

6. What is revocation of an offer?

7. What is meant by lapse of time in relation to an offer?

8. What is a unilateral contract?

9. What is meant by the postal rule?

10. Identify and explain the key cases related to offer and acceptance.

11. What is an implied term?

12. Identify the key implied terms under ss 12, 13, 14 and 15 of the Sale of Goods Act 1979. Describe a case which illustrates each of these implied terms.

13. Identify the key implied terms under ss 13, 14 and 15 of the Supply of Goods and Services Act 1982.

14. Under the Consumer Protection Act 1987, explain what is meant by a 'product', an 'own-brander' and 'damage'.

15. Identify seven things which an employer must notify to an employee when starting a new job.

16. Identify four duties of an employer and three duties of an employee under a contract of employment.

17. What is meant by vicarious liability and course of employment?

18. What is the difference between an employee and an independent contractor?

19. Identify three advantages of the principle of vicarious liability.

20. Identify the duties of both employer and employee under the Health and Safety at Work Act 1974.

21. Name the four main Acts of Parliament in the area of discrimination and outline the main provisions of each Act.

22. What is an employment tribunal?

23. What are the main advantages and disadvantages of using a tribunal rather than going to court?

24. Identify ten of the various rights and freedoms set out in the European Convention on Human Rights 1950.

25. Where is the European Court of Human Rights?

26. Briefly describe the significance of the Human Rights Act 1998 as far as enforcing the Convention is concerned.

27. Identify four restrictions on personal liberty recognised by English law.

28. Identify four restrictions on the right to freedom of speech (communication) recognised by English law.

29. Identify four different ways in which the right to a fair trial is protected by English law.

AQA Examination-style questions

■ Advice to candidates in GCSE Law examinations

Syllabus coverage

For you, that means making sure you have (effectively) revised all the key areas you will need for the examination. In this book, that means Chapters 1–5 and at least two (preferably more) of Chapters 6–9.

Answering the question

Read the question carefully. What exactly is the examiner asking for? Can I work out what is likely to be in the mark scheme? Can I reproduce that?

Relating the answer to the number of marks available

Both papers in the GCSE Law examination are 90 minutes long. Both Papers are marked out of 90. Therefore you should be thinking of about a mark a minute. Therefore a 5 mark answer should be briefer than a 10 mark answer.

Trigger words

Great care is exercised during the setting process to ensure that the question is prefaced by the appropriate 'trigger' word – name, state, identify, describe, discuss, comment on, etc. You should be aware that words such as "name", "state" and "identify" will require relatively little development. "Describe", "discuss" and "comment on" require a more in-depth approach.

The 'shopping list' answer

If the examiner has asked for three examples of something, don't write down five. There will almost certainly be a penalty if even one of your answers is wrong.

Citation of authority

If there is something you can use to support your answer (a case, Act of Parliament or an example). Use authority and you will gain extra credit.

Out-of-date material

Make sure what you revise and say in exams is up-to-date. In law, out-of-date material is just wrong.

Quality of written communication (QWC)

Do the obvious things. Start sentences with capital letters, finish with a full-stop and spell words correctly (especially specialist terms for your subject). About 5% of the marks are awarded for QWC!

Rubric infringement

Don't answer more than the required number of questions.

Commentary/evaluation questions

There is a simple rule which will attract more marks. If the question asks you to comment on/evaluate/ discuss the merits of something, look at both sides and draw a reasoned conclusion.

Answering problem questions

- Identify the relevant fact(s) from the problem.
- Identify the relevant issue raised.
- Quote relevant authority.
- Apply the law to the facts.
- Draw the appropriate conclusion.

General instructions to candidates

- Do complete personal and other details, including Centre and Candidate Numbers on page 1 of the Answer Booklet.
- If appropriate, write the question/sub-question number/letter in the left-hand margin. This will assist the examiner to fully credit the responses.
- Do try and write as neatly as possible, and, if you have time, go back and underline 'important' parts of your answer (but not in red).
- Do manage your time effectively. There are recommended times on the front of the question paper. Stick to them. Remember – a mark a minute.
- Do not use any colour other than black.
- Do not use correction fluid.
- Do not waste time by writing out the question, nor indeed waste further time by writing out all the relevant material in an area and then picking the right 'bit' for the answer. Answer the question as directly as you can.

AQA Examiner's tip

The rules that are set out here are largely commonsense. You will probably have heard teachers say many of the same things. What you probably do not realise is how important following these rules is. A candidate who follows these rules in an examination will probably score 10% more marks than a candidate who does not. Put another way, you will finish up with at least one grade higher (possibly more) just by following this advice. That sounds like a good deal!

Sample questions for Law Unit 1 (Section A)

1) Cases within the English legal system can be tried by different people. They include different judges such as District Judges, Circuit Judges, High Court Judges and Lords Justices of Appeal. Cases can also be decided by magistrates or juries sitting in different criminal courts.

In **each** of the following situations, identify **who** is most likely to be trying the case, and briefly explain **why**.

(a) Ivy, aged 16, has been charged with actual bodily harm (ABH) and is due in court next week. *(2 marks)*

(b) Josef has been accused of a serious assault on a teacher. At an initial hearing, the magistrates decided that the offence was too serious to be tried by magistrates. *(2 marks)*

(c) Keith bought a new fishing rod for £120 from *Anglers*, a shop which sells fishing equipment. Two weeks later, the rod snapped while Keith was using it. *Anglers* have refused to refund Keith's money. *(2 marks)*

 Examiner's tip Make a careful note of the different people who can deal with these cases. There are six in total. The answers to the three questions will be amongst those six named individuals.

2) Indicate whether each of the following statements is **true** or **false** by writing **TRUE** or **FALSE** in the space provided.

(a) Legal Help is a government-funded scheme used to give legal advice. ....

(b) Duty Solicitors can be used in both civil and criminal cases. ....

(c) Citizens Advice Bureaux are run by trained volunteers and give free advice. ....

(d) 'No win, no fee' arrangements are paid for by the government. ....

(e) Government-funded schemes for representation in court are all means-tested. ....

(5 marks)

3) In criminal cases, defendants who are found guilty can be punished in different ways. These punishments include:

• imprisonment for the most serious offences

• Community Orders (including Unpaid Work, Supervision, or Curfew Requirements) for offences which are serious enough to justify such orders

• fines or discharges for offences which are seen as less serious.

State which punishment may be imposed and briefly explain why.

(a) Ian, aged 22, has been arrested, for the third time, for driving whilst disqualified. This time, he was also found to be more than twice over the legal alcohol limit for driving. Ian intends pleading guilty to both offences at the Magistrates' Court. *(2 marks)*

Sample questions for Law Unit 1 (Section B)

Cases which are brought under English law can be heard either in the criminal or the civil court system. Civil cases, which are disputes between individuals, are generally heard either in the County Court or the High Court, with most being tried locally in the County Court. Cases in the County Court will be heard either by the Circuit Judge or District Judge, sitting alone. Alternatively, civil disputes can be resolved through the process of negotiation.

Criminal cases will be tried either in the Magistrates' Court or the Crown Court, depending on how serious the case is, how the accused decides to plead, and whether or not the magistrates feel they would have sufficient powers to sentence the accused.

Lay people play an important role in running the criminal justice system. Lay magistrates deal with most criminal cases which are tried by the criminal courts. In a trial in the Crown Court, the judge will sit with a jury of twelve ordinary members of the public. The jurors are chosen at random to try serious cases which have been committed or transferred from the Magistrates' Court.

(a) Outline the important differences between **civil** and **criminal** courts. *(4 marks)*

(b) Outline any two different types of case heard by the County Court. *(4 marks)*

(c) (i) Explain how, and in what circumstances, negotiation might be used as a method of dispute resolution. *(4 marks)*

    (ii) Comment on the advantages **and** disadvantages of a claim being settled by negotiation. *(4 marks)*

(d) Explain **three** differences between the Magistrates' Court and the Crown Court. *(6 marks)*

(e) Outline how lay magistrates are appointed. *(5 marks)*

(f) Describe how jurors qualify and are selected for jury service. *(5 marks)*

(g) Comment on how well each of the following carry out their role within the criminal justice system. (**Answer in continuous prose**.)

    (i) Lay magistrates *(5 marks)*

    (ii) Jurors. *(5 marks)*

Sample Question for Law Unit 2

There is a range of non-fatal offences against the person. They include:

- common assault (consisting of assault and battery) which is charged under the Criminal Justice Act 1988
- assault occasioning actual bodily harm under the Offences against the Person Act 1861
- grievous bodily harm and wounding, charged under two different sections of the 1861 Act.

The Problem

Len, aged 28, has had a history of violence since he was involved in a car accident seven years ago. He needed a blood transfusion but was unfortunately given blood from an infected donor. Len has since been diagnosed as HIV positive and has been on tablets ever since. This has kept him, physically, reasonably healthy but has had the effect of producing alarming mood swings and periods of depression. Len makes his situation worse by often getting drunk and he is also heavily into illegal drugs.

Maggie, Len's ex-girlfriend, has just been diagnosed as HIV positive. She was not aware at the time that Len was HIV positive. As they had had unprotected sex, she is certain that Len must have infected her, and done so deliberately. When she confronted Len, who was drunk at the time, he became verbally aggressive and hit her, causing bruising and a split lip.

Maggie reported these incidents to the police who went round to Len's house to make an arrest. Len again became aggressive and attacked the two officers. DS Nixon suffered a fractured skull and PC Ogden was cut across the face when Len threw a glass at her.

Len was arrested and has since been charged with several offences.

(a) (i) Discuss Len's criminal liability with respect to his aggressive behaviour and Maggie's injuries. *(6 marks)*

    (ii) Discuss Len's criminal liability with respect to Maggie contracting HIV. *(5 marks)*

(b) Identify and discuss the charge(s) that Len could face if Maggie dies from an HIV-related illness. *(6 marks)*

(c) Discuss what charges Len may face in respect of:

    (i) DS Nixon's fractured skull

    (ii) the injury to PC Ogden's face. *(6 marks)*

 Examiner's tip Read both the introductory material and the problem very carefully. The answers to some of the questions which follow can be found in the introduction, and you will need to apply that law to the facts of the problem.

Glossary

A

Acceptance: when the offeree (the person to whom the offer is made) agrees to the terms of the offer.

Act of God: an act of nature which could not have been foreseen.

Actionable *per se*: trespass does not require proof of damage by the claimant.

Administrator: a person appointed to deal with the estate of someone who has died intestate (i.e. without making a will) and who passes the estate to the beneficiaries (those entitled to the estate under the intestacy rules).

Advocate: someone who represents a client in court.

Aggravating: factors making the offence and sentence more severe.

Allurement: an attraction which tempts someone onto another's land.

Appellate court: a court which hears appeals.

Assault: an attempt or threat to apply force.

B

Banns: announcements in church of a forthcoming marriage.

Basic intent: crimes where the *mens rea* includes recklessness.

Battery: the application of force.

Beneficiary: someone who benefits from an estate under a will.

Bigamy: marrying someone whilst already married.

Binding precedent: a precedent which the judge must follow.

Bodily: in ABH/GBH this means harm to either body or mind.

Breach of the duty of care: where the defendant is negligent.

BWS: battered woman syndrome, affecting victims of long-term domestic abuse.

C

Case-hardened: magistrates may see the same types of case on a regular basis and may hear the same kinds of defences or excuses.

Chambers (judges): in the judge's room rather than in open court.

Chambers (barristers): offices, facilities and clerks shared by a group of barristers.

Claimant: the person bringing the civil court case.

Committee and amendments: detailed discussion/changes to the Bill.

Common law: judge-made, or case law.

Common law offence: one which is defined in case law rather than by Act of Parliament.

Consideration: what people give or promise under a contract.

Conversion: a permanent interference with someone's goods.

Conveyancing: buying and selling land.

Counsel: the name by which barristers are known.

Course of employment: an employee who is at work and doing his job (if this is the case, the employer is liable).

Court of first instance: a court where an original trial is heard.

D

Decree absolute: the end of the marriage.

Decree nisi: the provisional ending of a marriage.

Deferred: put off to a later time.

Direct intent: your aim, purpose or desire.

Discretionary: the judge has a choice.

Discrimination: treating someone unfairly because of their race, gender or disability.

Duty of care: a duty owed by the defendant.

E

Electoral register: electronic list of people registered to vote.

Euthanasia: where the defendant killed the victim at their own request, to avoid intense suffering due to a terminal illness.

Executor: personal representative named by the testator.

F

Family provision: provision which must be made for close family and dependants.

Fitness for purpose: goods able to do what is promised.

Forseeability: what the defendant should predict could happen.

G

Green/White Papers: Government publications before a Bill goes to Parliament.

Grievous: in GBH this means 'serious'.

I

ILEX fellows: a fellow of ILEX is a legal executive. They must be aged over 25 and pass Parts 1 and 2 of the ILEX exams and have been working in 'qualifying employment' for five years.

Implied term: a promise in a contract, not discussed by the parties.

Independent contractor: a person who has control over their own actions at work.

Indictable: the most serious type of crime: see classification chart.

Injunction: an order to stop doing something.

Invitation to treat: an invitation to make an offer.

Irretrievable breakdown: when a marriage cannot be saved.

J

Jury nobbling: threatening or bribing jurors.

Just, fair and reasonable: the defendant will only be liable if that is a fair outcome.

L

Law Commission: a body set up to advise the government on changes that need to be made to the law.

Lay person: not legally qualified or paid.

Leapfrogging: when the Court of Appeal is 'missed out', and the appeal is taken to the House of Lords directly from the High Court, as the House of Lords made the law that is the subject of the appeal.

Legislation/Act of Parliament/ Statute: these terms mean the same thing and are the end result of law-making by Parliament.

Litigation: the process of deciding an issue through a court case.

M

Maintenance: a financial settlement between the parties.

Mandatory: compulsory; the judge has no choice, as opposed to discretionary sentences, where they do.

Means tested: dependent on proof of low income and savings/investments.

Mediation: an out-of-court attempt to resolve issues between the parties.

Mitigating: factors making the offence and sentence less severe.

N

Necessity: committing a tort to prevent something worse.

A neighbour: a person who can be affected by the defendant's actions.

O

Obiter dicta: other comments made by judges.

Objective: seeing things from an independent or outside viewpoint.

Occasioning: in ABH this means 'causing'.

Offer: a statement of the terms by which the offeror (the person who makes the offer) is prepared to be bound.

P

Parliamentary supremacy (source of law): the principle that, under English Law, Parliament is the highest law-making body.

Parliamentary supremacy (human rights): the theory that all types of law are less important than Acts of Parliament and that Parliament can make any law it chooses.

Personal chattels: include personal property, but not money, shares or business property.

Persuasive precedent: a precedent which the judge may follow.

Perverse verdict: a verdict that goes against the evidence: voting with conscience.

Postal rule: the contract is complete as soon as the letter of acceptance is posted.

Precedent: a rule that later cases follow the principles in earlier cases.

Prescriptive right: a right acquired over time.

Private nuisance: interferes with an individual's right to enjoy their property.

Pro bono: for free.

Product: manufactured goods.

Prohibited degrees: close relations who cannot marry.

Proximity: how 'close' the defendant and claimant are, physically or emotionally.

Public bodies: any organisation serving a government purpose or public function, e.g. local authorities, the courts, police service, prison service, etc.

Public nuisance: affects a large group of people.

R

R: Regina (the Queen), in whose name the prosecution is brought.

Ratio decidendi: the reason for a decision.

Readings: Parliament discussing the Bill.

Reasonable man: the standard against which the defendant's conduct is judged.

Recklessness: foresight of a risk, but carrying on anyway.

Recorder: an experienced barrister or solicitor-advocate who works as a part-time judge for 15–30 days per year.

Regulations and Directives: different forms of EU Law.

Remoteness of damage: the rule that a claimant cannot recover damages if his loss could not have been foreseen.

Res ipsa loquitur: an obvious case of negligence where the defendant has to prove he was not negligent.

Revocation: changing or disposing of a will.

Rights of audience: the authority to represent clients in court.

Royal Assent: the Queen's permission for the Bill to become an Act.

S

Sales by sample: inspect a small quantity and buy a large quantity.

Satisfactory quality: the standard of goods one would expect to receive.

Source: where the law comes from/how it is made.

Specific intent: crimes where a specific intent (not recklessness) is required, e.g. murder intent to kill.

State: defined territory covered by a system of government, e.g. the UK.

Statutory trusts: an equal division of the estate between the children of the deceased either on their 18th birthday or on a prior marriage.

Stigma: bad reputation because of society's disapproval.

Subjective: based on view of an individual/group.

Subjective: seeing things from an inside/personal viewpoint.

Summary: the least serious type of crime.

T

Testator: the person who makes a will.

Tort: a civil wrong such as negligence, nuisance, trespass.

Trespass to goods: a minor interference with someone's goods.

Trespasser: someone unlawfully on another's land.

Triable-either-way: mid-range crimes: see classification chart.

Tribunal: a body which deals with disputes in employment.

Trivial: only slight injury, e.g. red face, minor scratches or bruises.

A trust: an obligation to administer property for another/others.

U

Unanimous: all agree with the decision.

V

Vicarious liability: an employer's liability for the actions of an employee.

Vicarious liability: an employer's responsibility for the actions of an employee.

Visitor: a person lawfully on another's land.

Void marriage: a marriage that has never existed.

Voidable marriage: a marriage that can be annulled (ended) by a court order – not to be confused with the dissolution (ending) of a marriage by divorce.

Volenti non fit injuria: the defence of consent.

Index